HOW TO FORMAT WORD DOCS LIKE A PRO

SECOND EDITION

DAWN GREENFIELD IRELAND

ARTISTIC ORIGINS

CONTENTS

How to Format Word Docs Like A Pro Second Edition by Dawn Greenfield Ireland

Published by Artistic Origins

https://www.dawngreenfieldireland.com/artistic-origins

ISBN 9781940385945 (eBook) Second Edition 8/23/2025

ISBN 9781940385952 (paperback) Second Edition 8/23/2025

Book formatted by Yours Truly (me)

Dawn Greenfield Ireland
Artistic Origins Inc.
www.degreenfield.com

Please visit my website: www.degreenfield.com and sign up for my newsletter and get the latest news before the public.

Be kind = leave a review!

I created the Living Smart Series to teach people what I've learned over the years—things I'm good at. Everyone should have access to knowledge that can help them get ahead.

— Dawn Greenfield Ireland

LIVING SMART SERIES

ACKNOWLEDGMENTS

A great cover says it all. Many thanks to Brandon White for creating the cover for the second edition.

Sandy Penny, editor extraordinaire, has eyes like laser pinpoints! She whacked me a couple of times!

A fabulous review says it all. Richard P. Stone, aka Grasshopper, aka Dickie, took my online class for this book. He is a novice Word user, so his comments were a strong testament for the program which is updated to match the book at various times.

> As a retired teacher, I was impressed by Dawn's teaching style in her videos of "How to Format Word Docs Like a Pro". As a beginning writer, I found it very easy to learn the ways of writing, thanks to Dawn.
>
> She ran her tutorials like she was in the classroom. She would state the objective of the lesson. Then taught the objective through her easy-to-follow visuals of different types of writing. Then she would take the objective a step further by explaining why things go wrong and the reasons for the mistakes. Dawn shows you the potholes of writing without falling into them.
>
> Her patience along with her ability to communicate her

points of instruction was never confusing or talking over my head. Her tutorials gave me confidence that I can overcome my most basic fears of writing.

I strongly recommend this class for all writers who seek the proper way of getting their work out there.

Richard P. Stone
Author, *Survivors of the Mutant Dawn*

INTRODUCTION

Welcome to *How to Format Word Docs Like A Pro, Second Edition* so you can create great-looking professional documents.

I know you had a lot of choices, so I would like to thank you for choosing my book.

If you want to watch the video as you read the book, the online course is fast-tracked and self-paced.

There are quite a few features in a word processing program, and most people don't know how to make their documents look attractive. Sometimes, it isn't even obvious how to find the tool you need in the program.

You will notice I suggest you hunt things down via Google or YouTube. There are many versions of MS Word out there. Things I discuss may be in a different location than what you see on the screenshots in this book, or not available at all if your version of Word is old and you have not updated the program consistently.

Also, I won't know if you are on a PC or a Mac. Don't be discouraged. You will be able to learn everything I present in the book.

Whether you need professional documents for your job, your business, a hobby, or a neighborhood association, this book will show you how to create professional-looking documents you can be proud of.

Don't worry if you are not a big power Microsoft Word user.

That's what you're here for. This book is going to separate you from the people in your organization. By the time you finish digesting this content, you will have skills other office workers don't have.

You may discover your colleagues and co-workers will depend on you to fix their documents—you'll become the Word Doctor in your office. It's an easy process once the mystery is removed. You might even rise up that corporate ladder.

The content in this book is identical to my online course. In both, I have broken down what you will walk away with.

Here's what you'll learn:

- How to use Styles
- Format Titles and Section Titles
- Format Paragraphs and Bullets
- Automate First Line Indents so you never have to Tab over
- Set up Spacing before and after Lists or Screenshots
- Automatically generate a Table of Contents
- Create a New Style from scratch
- Create a Template
- Why you should love the Pilcrow mark
- How to use and understand Track Changes
- How to Resize an image (graphic or screenshot)

Once you finish reading this book you are going to be a different person.

Do you know why? Because everything you were afraid of that stopped you from learning new skills to begin with won't even be relevant anymore. You will have abilities that will stay with you throughout your entire career.

The online class does not have an expiration date. You will be able to watch the video course as many times as you want. https://www.degreenfield.com/online-courses

Sign up for my newsletter on my website so you know when I create another book that might help you in your personal life and/or your career.

My website address is http://degreenfield.com/

LESSON 1: YOUR VERSION OF MS WORD

Having a good command of MS Word is a prized skill. You are going to learn how to use Styles to transform documents. Styles are the core of using MS Word fully and properly.

With a little practice, you will be able to format titles, paragraphs, bullets and a lot of other things. I'll show you how to generate a table of contents from your headings, how to create a new style from scratch, and even how to create a template. You will also learn how important the pilcrow mark plays in your quest for perfect documentation.

These things will help you in your day job, your organization, or may even help you get a better job.

Functional Menus

Before we start to work on creating a good-looking document,

I'm going to identify some items and the terms I'll be using to make it easier for you to follow along.

When you open a document in Word, or create a New document, the tabs across the top contain **functional menus**. They are somewhat the same in Pages for Mac.

If your document header doesn't look like this picture, check YouTube or Google for your version of MS Word to find things that I will point out that are not in the same place on your computer.

Find Your Version of Word

You can find your version of Word here at the top of your screen.

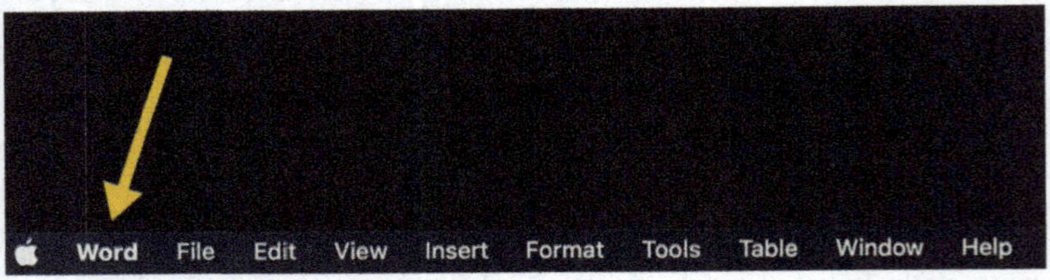

Click on Word. The following drop-down menu appears.

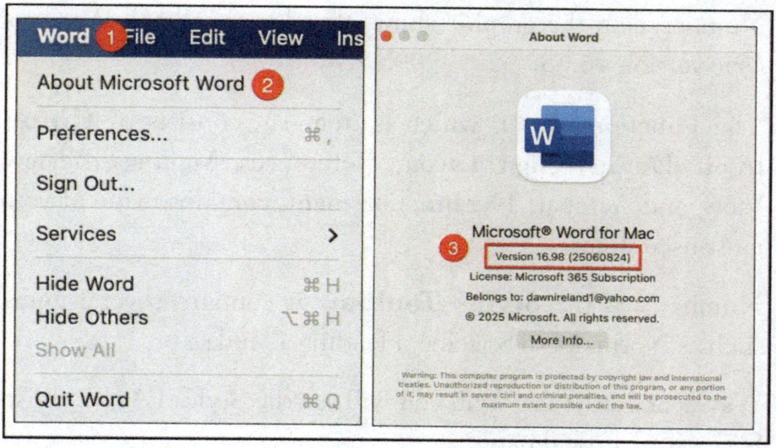

Click #2, the first item in the menu, About Microsoft Word.

#3 shows the version of the program on your computer.

If you do not update your program when a new version is released, the program might not function properly, or you will miss out on updated features and fixed program bugs.

This next screenshot identifies the top of the page in Word. I've added my version of Word from the above screen captures in case it differs from your program.

1. My program is MS Word for Mac V 16.89
2. The HOME tab
3. Styles Toolbar
4. Styles Pane

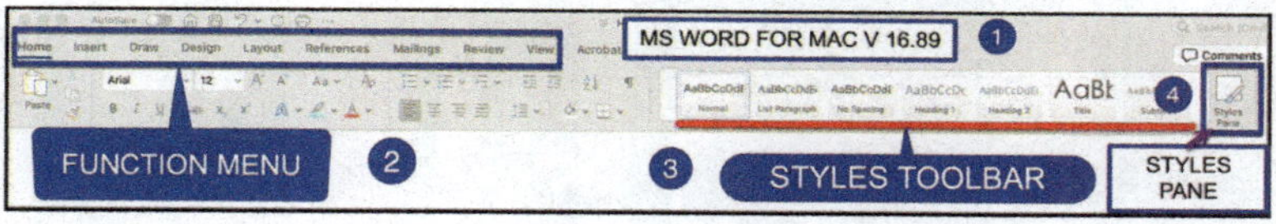

Number 1 on the graphic shows that I'm using MS Word for Mac version 16.98.

The Function Menu, which is item #2, consists of **Home**, Insert, Draw, Design, Layout, References, Mailings, Review, View, and Acrobat. The function menu contains many of your most-used items.

Number 3 is the **Styles Toolbar.** It contains several items, such as Normal, No Spacing, Heading 1, and so on.

Way over on the far-right, you will see the Styles PANE. It lists Styles in a vertical pane.

Let's get started so you can learn some tips and tricks in MS Word. In this lesson, you will learn how to transform this clump of words into a great-looking document.

Just so you know, I'm using text from one of my other online classes, Writers' Preparation Handbook. This example may be too small to read here, but you will find a full-page version in the back of the book.

Does this example look anything like some documents you have seen, or even created in the past?

Here's why the Writers' Preparation Handbook course is for you:
You want to write a book, but you don't know the first thing about getting started. Will it cost you money to create a book? How should you begin? Maybe you're not that computer
savvy. This course helps you get everything organized so when you sit down in front of that computer you will not be intimidated by the setup and mechanics of getting started. You will be able to dive into writing your book content and, you will make great progress as you challenge yourself to write more and more each time you sit down at your computer. The great thing is, you will learn some neat tips and tricks along the way to make your book dream come true.
Some of the things you will learn are:
* Why you should test the waters with an eBook
* How to organize your new writingbusiness
* How to make project folders and subfolders
* How to protect your work and your computer equipment
* Why you should research characters' professions
* How to know your locations if you live somewhere else
* How to set up your working file
* What are Styles?
* Don't do that manually!
* Where is that thing?
* Why join a Critique Group
What are the requirements for this course?
First and foremost, you should have the desire to write a book. While you can use a pen and paper, it is highly advisable to use a computer with a word processing program because writing the book is only the first part of your journey.
What am I going to get from this course?
This course will prepare you so you can sit down and begin the organization of your book and start writing. Who is the target audience?
This course is for anyone who has an idea for a book, or someone who has already written a book but it has been sitting in a drawer on hold because they didn't know how to proceed. And anyone who needs a refresher course.

You will notice there are no paragraph indents or separations. Everything is up against the left margin. Where does one sentence begin and the next thought end?

All the bullets are flush to the left with little stars, called asterisks, used for bullets.

There is no paragraph spacing above or below the bullets, so you never notice there are two Section Titles in this big mess.

You will be proud of the document you create after learning several Word secrets.

This clump of words is actually a description of the course, but you'd never guess that because of the way it's presented here. People will want to know how they will benefit from taking this course, so that first line in the clump of words should stand alone and be centered.

First, I'm going to delete the colon after "you" in the screenshot.

Here's why the Writers' Preparation Handbook course is fo you:

Delete the colon

You want to write a book, but you don't know the first thing about getting started. Will it cost you money to create a book? How should you begin? Maybe you're not that computer
savvy. This course helps you get everything organized so when you sit down in front of that computer you will not be intimidated by the setup and mechanics of getting started. You will be able to dive into writing your book content and, you will make great progress as you challenge yourself to write more and more each time you sit down at your computer. The great thing is, you will learn some neat tips and tricks along the way to make your book dream come true.

LESSON 2: STYLES AND FORMATTING

The Styles Toolbar and Styles Pane

As I mentioned earlier, **Styles** are the core of using Word fully and properly.

I will teach you how to apply a Style to the title of the document.

The current style in the **Styles toolbar, #1 in the screenshot** is Normal.

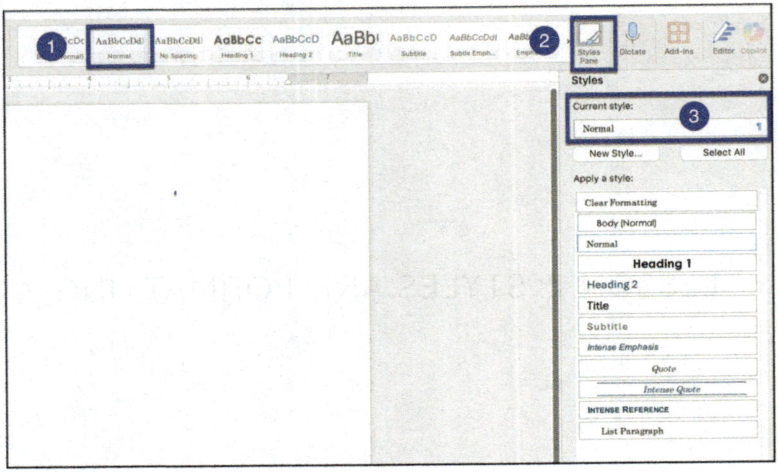

When you click on the **Styles Pane, #2,** it opens a panel to the right of your document body and shows a list of styles that are available. The style Normal is shown in **#3**.

For this exercise, you will learn how to use the Styles Pane to modify a style. This is the better option to get exactly what you want.

We want to modify the title so it stands out on the page.

Scroll down until you find **#1**, **Title** in the Styles Panel.

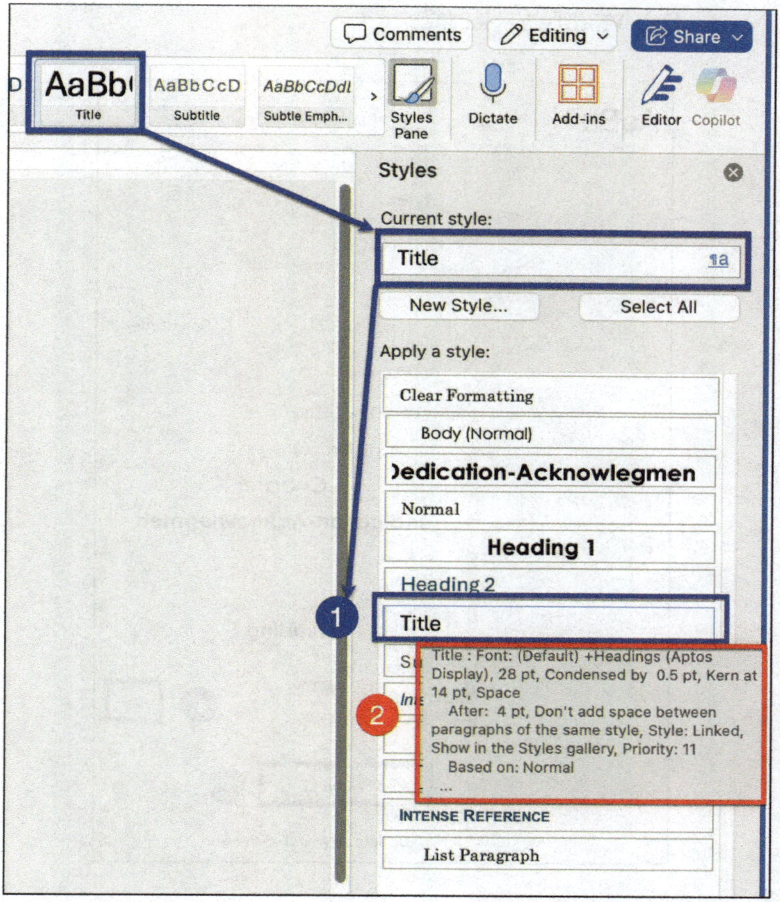

When you hover your mouse over the style named Title, the **default settings #2** become visible. This shows you the font size, spacing and other default settings.

Think of defaults as someone's used furniture.

We will now Modify this style.

Click the **down** arrow**, #1**, that becomes visible when your mouse hovers over the style Title.

Next, click Modify Style, **#2.**

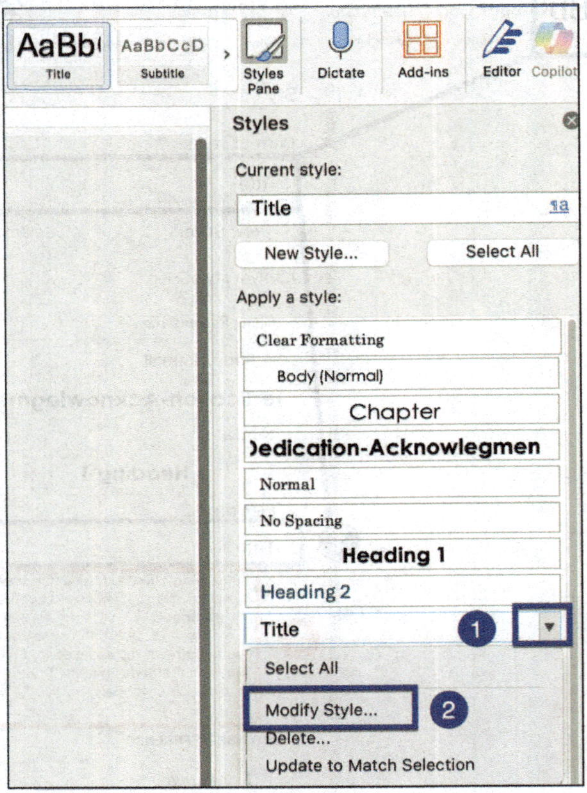

The Modify Style box opens. Take the time to study this box.

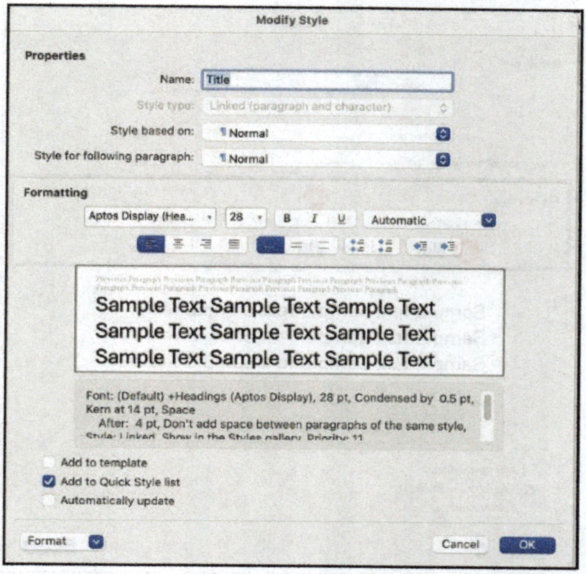

Modify Style is like getting the keys to a document candy shop. You can modify everything until it looks exactly like you want it to.

On the next screen, **#1** iYs where you can change the font by choosing a different font name, font size, and color.

You can also set up whether you want the title to be bold, italicized, or underlined.

Modify settings allows you to change the position of the word on the page from right, left, centered or justified, **#2**.

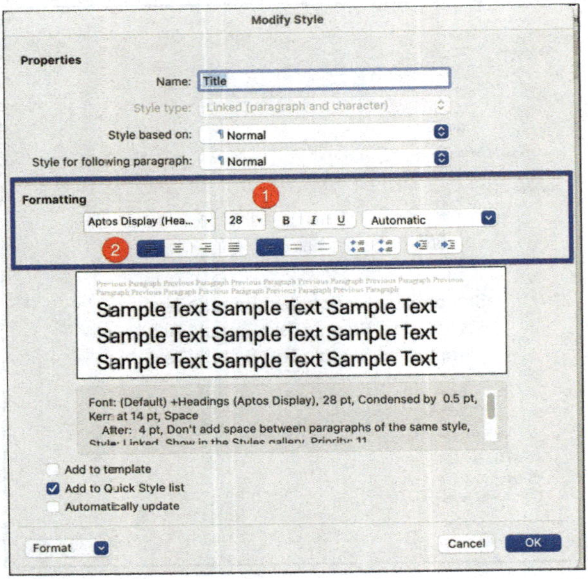

Changing Fonts and Spacing

To change the font to Century Gothic (one of my favorite fonts), click the down arrow where you see the name of the font, **#1**.

Since this is a title, lets keep the same size, 28, because that's a good size for the title of this document.

Change the position of the title so it will be centered on the page, **#2**.

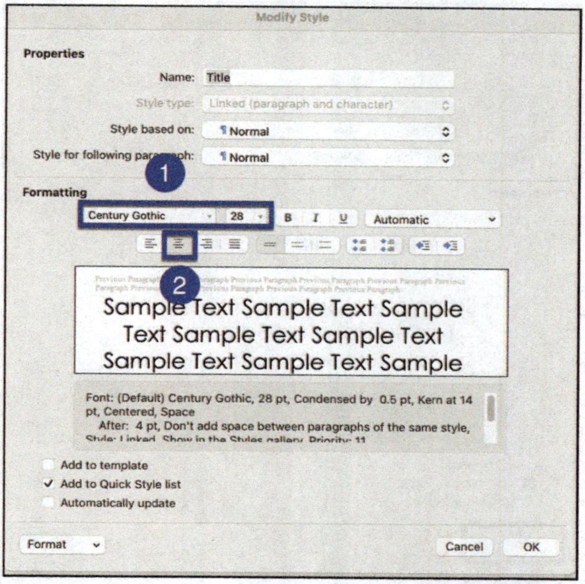

Adequate spacing should separate the first paragraph from the title.

In the next image, click on the down arrow, **#1** beside Format.

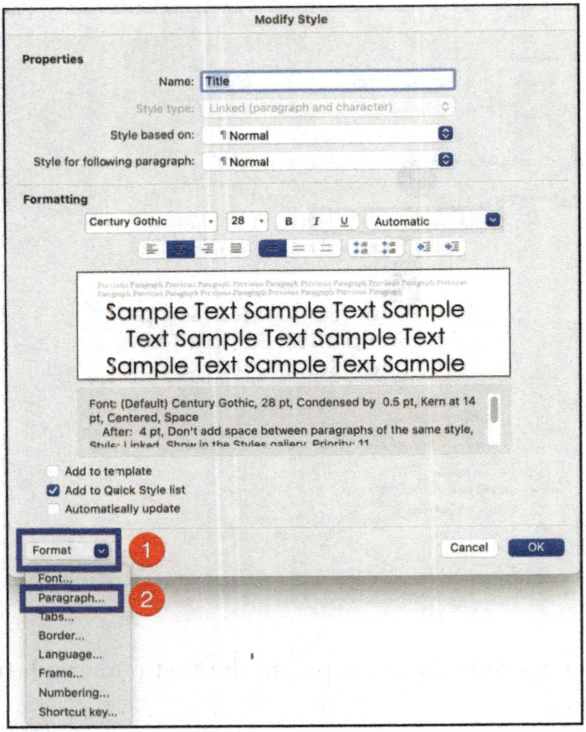

Choose Paragraph, **#2**.

In the next screenshot, the Paragraph box opens.

Click on **#1**, Spacing. In the spacing area click the **up arrow #2** in the **After** box. I have changed the After Spacing to 30.

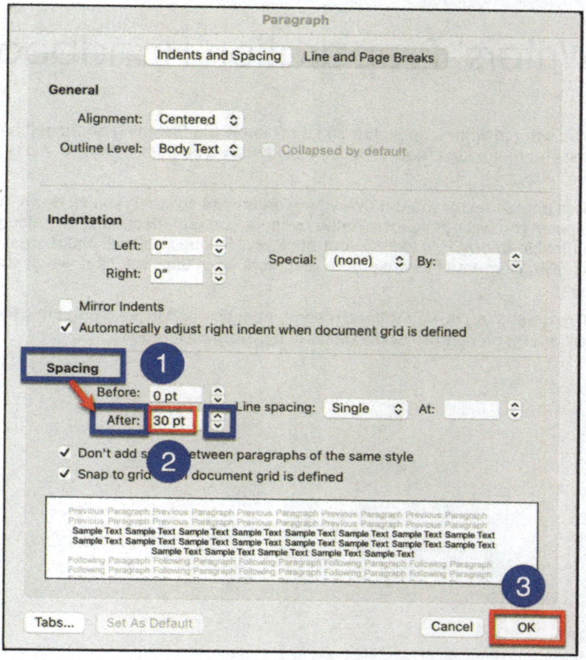

Click OK, **#3**.

Always click OK to save your changes.

There is now generous space between the title and first paragraph, as shown in the next screenshot.

Writers' Preparation Handbook

You want to write a book, but you don't know the first thing about getting started. Will it cost you money to create a book? How should you begin? Maybe you're not that computer savvy.

This course helps you get everything organized so when you sit down in front of that computer you will not be intimidated by the setup and mechanics of getting started. You will be able to dive into writing your book content, and you will make great progress as you challenge yourself to write more and more each time you sit down at your computer.

The great thing is, you will learn some neat tips and tricks along the way to make your book dream come true. Some of the things you will learn are:

LESSON 3: MODIFY STYLE

Identifying Paragraphs, Bullets and Section Titles

Let's examine that clump of words again and identify the features of this document. I have color-coded this example to help you identify the features that are all clumped together.

Paragraphs highlighted in yellow.

Bullets are an aqua blue color.

Section Titles are magenta/pink.

You will recognize these features with the color coding shown in upcoming lessons.

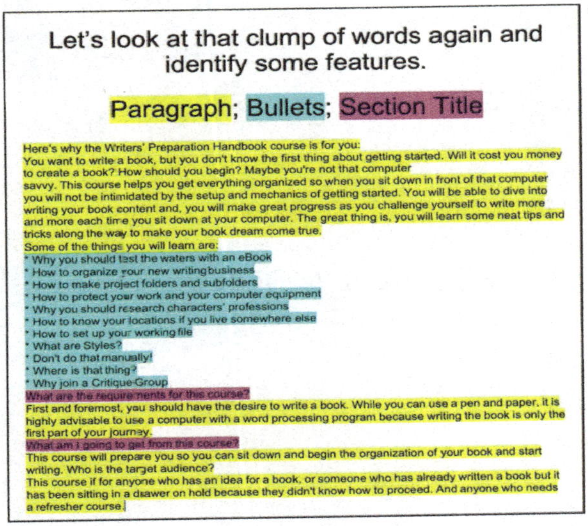
Let's look at that clump of words again and identify some features.

Paragraph; Bullets; Section Title

Here's why the Writers' Preparation Handbook course is for you:
You want to write a book, but you don't know the first thing about getting started. Will it cost you money to create a book? How should you begin? Maybe you're not that computer
savvy. This course helps you get everything organized so when you sit down in front of that computer you will not be intimidated by the setup and mechanics of getting started. You will be able to dive into writing your book content and, you will make great progress as you challenge yourself to write more and more each time you sit down at your computer. The great thing is, you will learn some neat tips and tricks along the way to make your book dream come true.
Some of the things you will learn are:
* Why you should test the waters with an eBook
* How to organize your new writing business
* How to make project folders and subfolders
* How to protect your work and your computer equipment
* Why you should research characters' professions
* How to know your locations if you live somewhere else
* How to set up your working file
* What are Styles?
* Don't do that manually!
* Where is that thing?
* Why join a Critique Group
What are the requirements for this course?
First and foremost, you should have the desire to write a book. While you can use a pen and paper, it is highly advisable to use a computer with a word processing program because writing the book is only the first part of your journey.
What am I going to get from this course?
This course will prepare you so you can sit down and begin the organization of your book and start writing. Who is the target audience?
This course if for anyone who has an idea for a book, or someone who has already written a book but it has been sitting in a drawer on hold because they didn't know how to proceed. And anyone who needs a refresher course.

Headings are an important feature in Styles. When you apply them correctly in your document, headings build your table of contents.

Section Title should be smaller than the document title.

In the big clump that is our document, there are two hidden section titles among the crowded text. See **#1** in the screenshot.

To apply the Heading 1 Style to the **Section Titles** of the Document, click **#2**, Styles Pane, to open the panel.

Go to **Heading 1** in the panel, **#3** on the screenshot.

Click the down arrow, **#4.**

Then click **Modify Style**, **#5**.

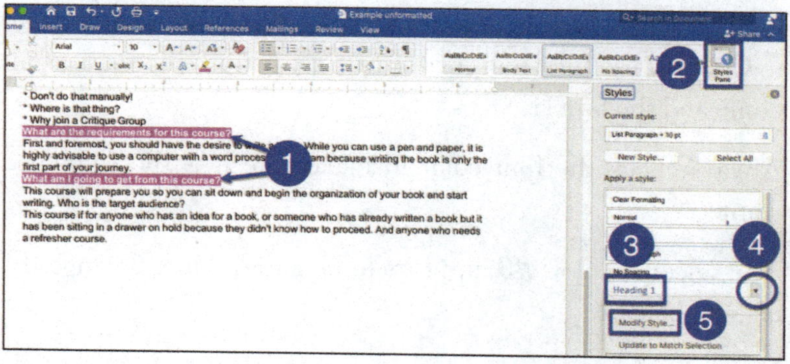

The **Modify Style** screen, **#1** on the following screen capture, is where we will apply formatting.

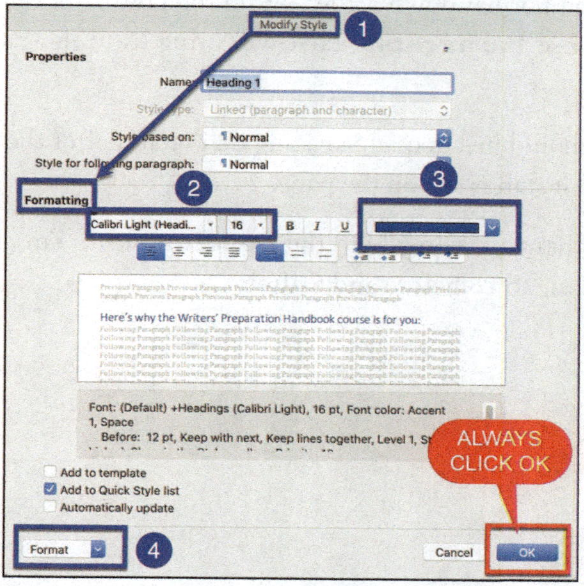

Since the **Document Title** font is Century Gothic 28, the **Section Title** should be smaller.

Currently, the font is set to the default, **#2**. To change the font to Century Gothic 16 in the formatting section, choose the font name and the font size.

Always check the font color to make sure it is the color you want.

The selected color, **#3**, appears to be a dark blue. Change the color to black.

Next, change the paragraph formatting so that the Section Title stands out.

Are you catching on to this?

Click the Format down arrow **#4** on the bottom of that screen and choose **Paragraph**. That will bring us to the Paragraph box.

There should be adequate spacing before and after the Section Title, so it stands out on the page.

Those changes are made in the **Spacing** block. I'm changing the spacing to 18 before and 6 after.

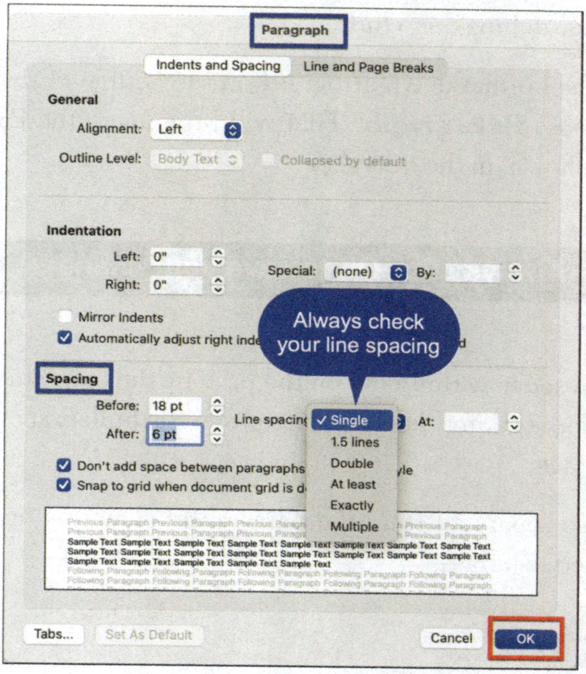

Line Spacing

Always check the Line spacing to make sure it is set correctly as there are multiple choices:

- Single
- 1.5 lines
- Double
- At least
- Exactly
- Multiple

Next, change the paragraph formatting so that the Section Title stands out.

Are you catching on to this?

Click the Format down arrow **#4** on the bottom of that screen and choose **Paragraph**. That will bring us to the Paragraph screen shown on the next slide.

Always click OK to save your changes.

You can see how this looks on the page by the light blue shaded area. The section title is separated from the bullets above it by a large space.

It is also separated from the paragraph below it so it's not all crammed together.

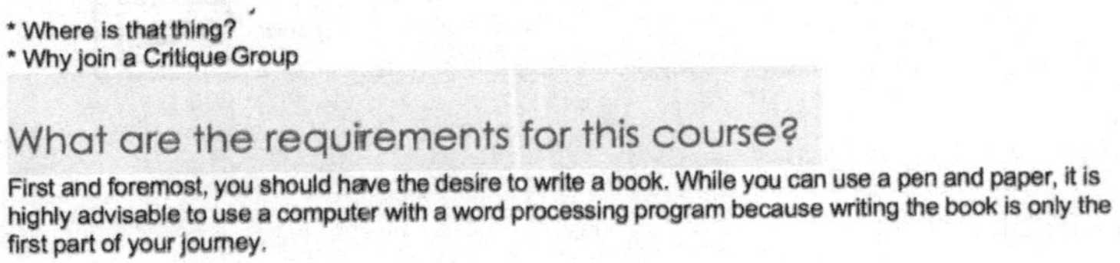
* Where is that thing?
* Why join a Critique Group

What are the requirements for this course?

First and foremost, you should have the desire to write a book. While you can use a pen and paper, it is highly advisable to use a computer with a word processing program because writing the book is only the first part of your journey.

From this point on, anytime you come across a **Section Title** in this document, you can click on **Heading 1** in the toolbar instead of going to the Styles Pane.

When you change a style's default, the new style attributes will be available in the style in the Styles toolbar.

Now let's tackle the paragraph text. A paragraph should be about one idea. We will use **Normal** for the style in the Styles

Pane, then change the paragraph defaults to what we want for that style.

Some people write with one gigantic paragraph on a page. That looks like a big block of black ink that is difficult to read.

Everything should be broken down into logical, readable paragraphs with enough white-space on the page so the reader can discern where a new paragraph begins.

Indents and Paragraphs

There are two ways of breaking down paragraphs into readable chunks. You can automate your first line of a paragraph with an indent, or you can leave a blank line between paragraphs.

A standard indent is five spaces, or half an inch (0.5"). If you are of an age where you learned to type on a typewriter and didn't have a tab key, you would spacebar over five spaces to create the indent. The tab key is set at the standard five spaces.

Do you see the block that says Indentation, **#1**? That's where we will set up the First line indent.

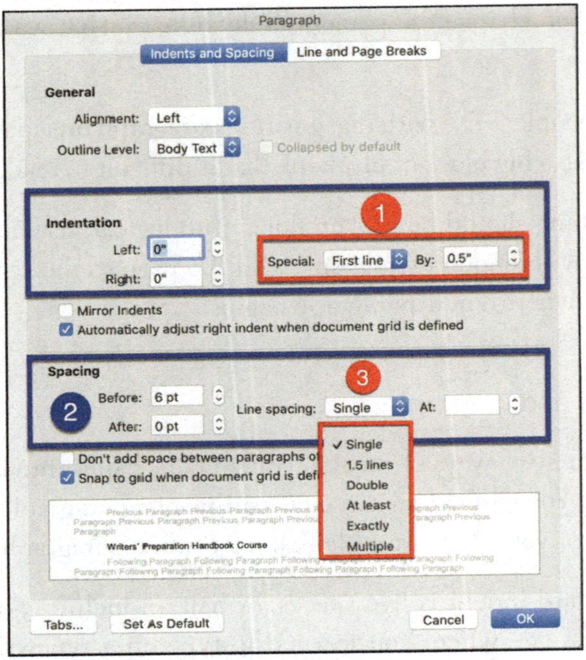

As you can see here on the screenshot, indentation is set to the standard 0.5" (five manual spaces using your spacebar), which is half an inch.

By setting the First Line Indentation, you are **automating** this function so you don't have to use your tab key.

Next, we will set the spacing between paragraphs, **#2**.

I'm using my standard 6 points **Before**. You can increase that to make your paragraph spaces larger. Experiment with changing the After spacing.

Depending on your document, you may also want to change the Line Spacing from single to 1-1/2 lines or double spacing. There are options to wiggle the spacing using At Least, Exactly, and Multiple.

If you do not want to indent paragraphs, **do not choose** the First line indentation setting, seen in screenshot, **#1**.

NOTE: if you don't indent, you will need to hit your Return/Enter key to leave a blank line between paragraphs, otherwise you will end up with that big, black crammed-looking page.

Here's what our paragraph changes look like.

You want to write a book, but you don't know the first thing about getting started. Will it cost you money to create a book? How should you begin? Maybe you're not that computer savvy.

This course helps you get everything organized so when you sit down in front of that computer you will not be intimidated by the setup and mechanics of getting started. You will be able to dive into writing your book content and, you will make great progress as you challenge yourself to write more and more each time you sit down at your computer.

The great thing is, you will learn some neat tips and tricks along the way to make your book dream come true. Some of the things you will learn are:

Bullets

Now, for those ugly bullets. Word processing programs have a built-in Bullet feature where you can choose the style of bullets. Originally, the bullets are shown as asterisks (little stars), instead of traditional bullets.

First, highlight the list of bullets.

*Why you should test the waters with an eBook
*How to organize your new writing business
*How to make project folders and subfolders

*How to protect your work and your computer equipment
*Why you should research characters' professions
*How to know your locations if you live somewhere else
*How to set up your working file
*What are Styles?
*Don't do that manually!
*Where is that thing?
*Why join a Critique Group

Then click **Bullets** in the toolbar.

Choose what style of bullet you want to use here. For this example, we are going to use the standard round bullet.

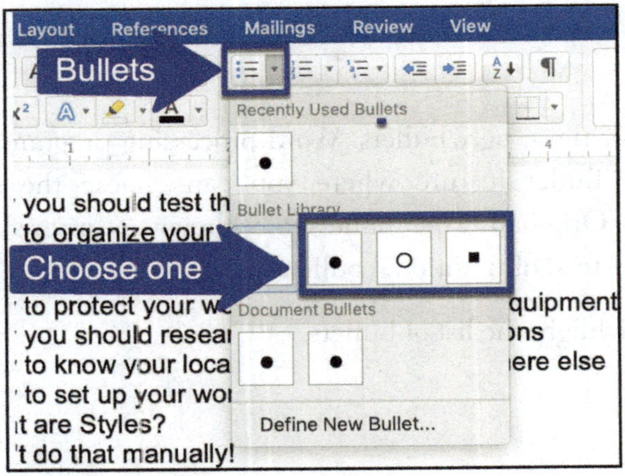

The spacing between bullets is off. Did you see the blank line between the 3rd and 4th bullets? Do you know what to do to fix this?

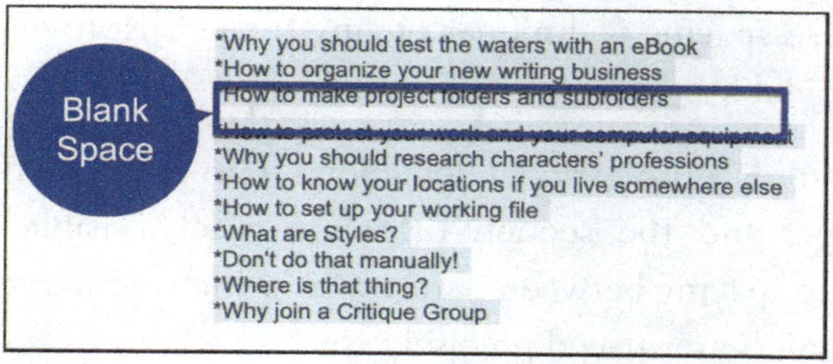

1. Click Format Paragraph.
2. Make sure the spacing is set to **Single**. You can adjust the spacing so there is 0 spacing before and after, or the amount of spacing you like.

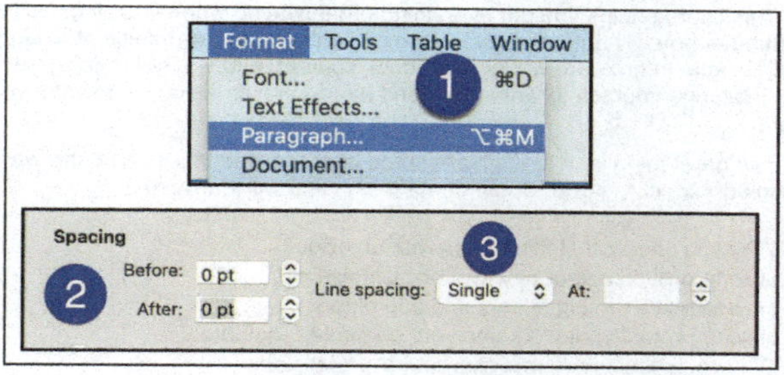

Now your bullets are uniform in style.

- Why you should test the waters with an eBook
- Organize your new writing business
- Make project folders and subfolders
- Protect your work and your computer equipment
- Research characters' professions
- Know your locations
- Setting up your working file
- Learn and use Styles
- Don't do that manually!
- Where is that thing?
- Critique Groups

Use these spacing techniques on any type of list to make them more readable.

The result is a professional document. The Title is centered on the page, and the section titles are nicely visible. There's adequate spacing between paragraphs, which are indented, and those bullets are spaced precisely.

Writers' Preparation Handbook

You want to write a book, but you don't know the first thing about getting started. Will it cost you money to create a book? How should you begin? Maybe you're not that computer savvy.

This course helps you get everything organized so when you sit down in front of that computer you will not be intimidated by the setup and mechanics of getting started. You will be able to dive into writing your book content, and you will make great progress as you challenge yourself to write more and more each time you sit down at your computer.

The great thing is, you will learn some neat tips and tricks along the way to make your book dream come true. Some of the things you will learn are:

- Why you should test the waters with an eBook
- How to organize your new writing business
- How to make project folders and subfolders
- How to protect your work and your computer equipment
- Why you should research characters' professions
- How to know your locations if you live somewhere else
- How to set up your working file
- What are Styles?
- Don't do that manually!
- Where is that thing?
- Why join a Critique Group

What are the requirements for this course?

First and foremost, you should have the desire to write a book. While you can use a pen and paper, it is highly advisable to use a computer with a word processing program because writing the book is only the first part of your journey.

What am I going to get from this course?

This course will prepare you so you can sit down and begin the organization of your book and start writing.

Who is the target audience?

This course if for anyone who has an idea for a book, or someone who has already written a book but it has been sitting in a drawer on hold because they didn't know how to proceed. And anyone who needs a refresher course.

More Bullet Fixes

There are more ways to adjust bullets.

Highlight the bullets as shown in #1. Notice the Indents in the ruler area in #2.

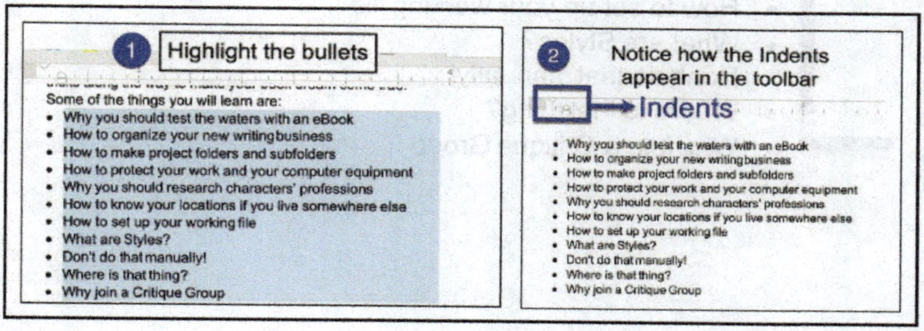

Experiment how to move the top and bottom Indents, #3. These two little indent tabs move independently.

You can see how the indents have changed from the left margin to about the quarter of an inch point on the ruler.

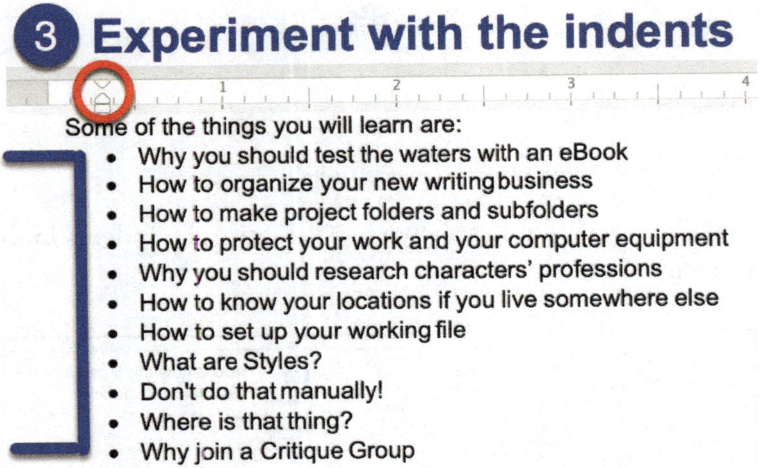
3
Experiment with the indents
1
2
3
4
Some of the things you will learn are:
Why you should test the waters with an eBook
How to organize your new writing business
How to make project folders and subfolders
How to protect your work and your computer equipment
Why you should research characters' professions
How to know your locations if you live somewhere else
How to set up your working file
What are Styles?
Don't do that manually!
Where is that thing?
Why join a Critique Group

LESSON 4: GENERATE A TABLE OF CONTENTS

Let's talk about a Table of Contents. Depending on the type of book you are writing you might want to include a preface, introduction, dedication or acknowledgment page. Many authors include other books by to let the buyer know there's more where this came from. These pages go in the front of the book after the copyright page and the table of contents.

Also included in the table of contents will be pages in the back of the book, such as About the Author. If this was a novel, you might have a snippet about the next book in the series. If this is a business/nonfiction book, there may be a glossary, acronym list, or references.

The images on this page are the table of contents for Mastering Your Money. While it's a small book, it has a generous TOC so the reader can find what he's looking for at a glance

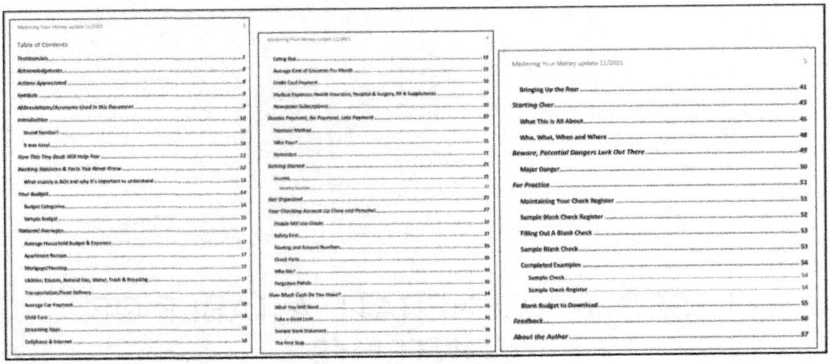
Table of Contents

Mastering Your Money update 11/2021 5

NOTE: Never, ever create a manual Table of Contents.

When you let the word processing program generate the TOC, you won't have to worry about accidentally choosing the wrong font name or size, or getting all your entries aligned correctly, or making sure the page numbers are correct.

The automatically generated TOC is also helpful when you add a new chapter, rearrange chapters, change titles, or correct errors in your titles. Chapter numbers will automatically renumber themselves (thank you!) when rearranged in your document.

A table of contents should always start on a blank page after the copyright page and before the body of your document. It could span multiple pages, depending on the size of your document and the number of sections.

Install A Page Break

If you have not upgraded to Office 365, I will call this the ORIGINAL MS Word screen. Click the Insert tab above the toolbar, which is #1 in the screenshot.

Click the down arrow beside Pages, which is #2.

Click #3, Page Break. A page break will insert a blank page in your document.

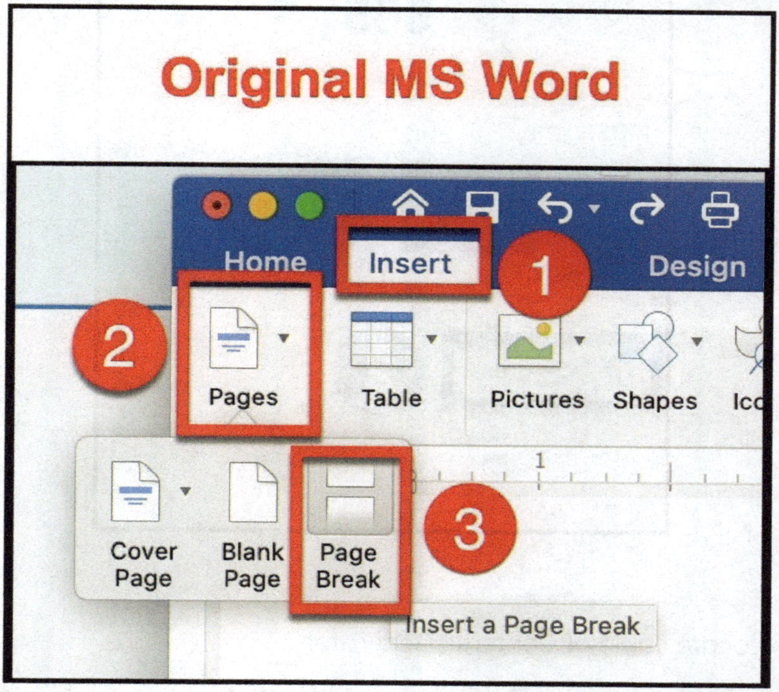

For Word in Office 365 there are only 2 steps.

Click the Insert tab above the toolbar, which is #1 in the screenshot.

Click #2, Page Break. A page break will insert a blank page in your document.

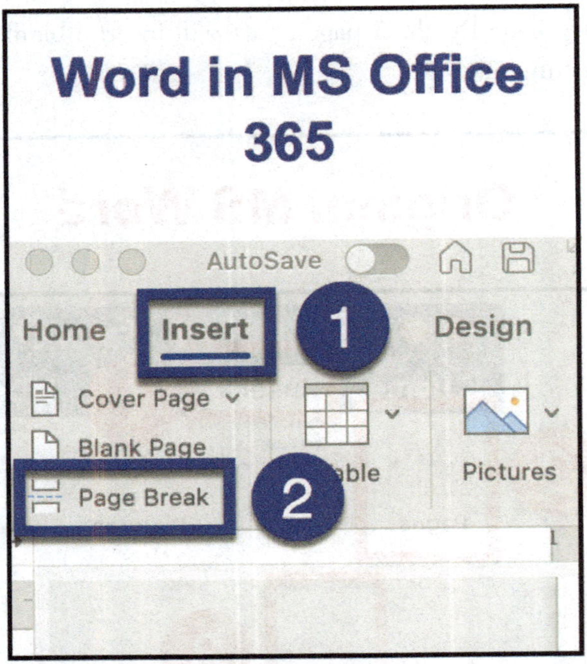

Locate Table of Contents Generator

At the top of the blank page, go to the **References tab, #1** over the toolbar.

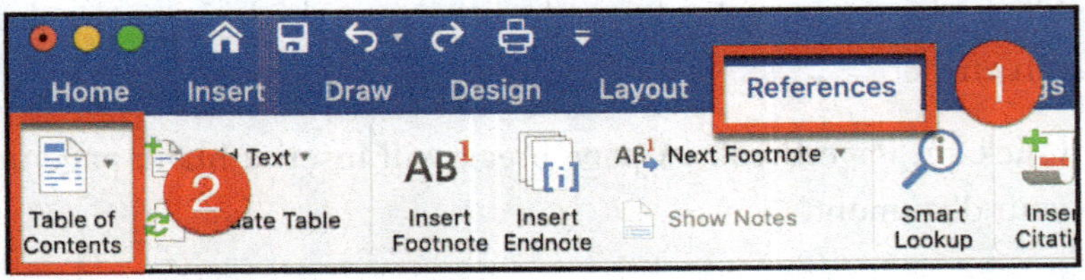

Find **Table of Contents, #2**, which is typically over on the left side of the menu, and click the down arrow.

Let's look at the Automatic Table of Contents, which is #1 in the graphic.

Make sure you scroll down to see all the different styles, which is #2 in the screenshot. You can choose from Classic, Contemporary, Formal, Modern and Simple.

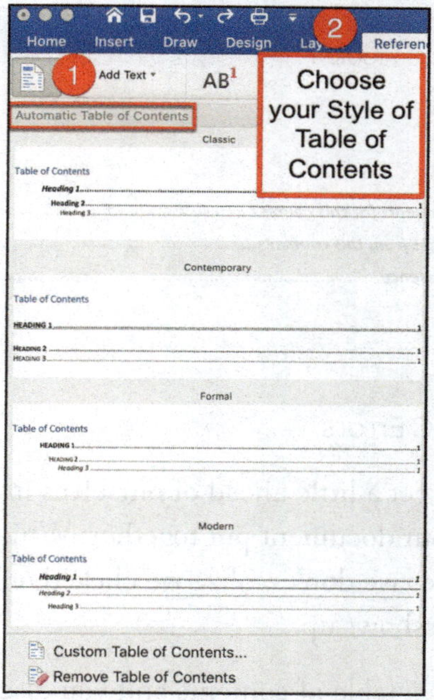

Choose the style of TOC that is appropriate for your document, or what your client specifies.

While you have the option to choose a Manual Table of Contents, I don't recommend it.

That entails manually typing in your section titles and page numbers. That could turn into a nightmare if you use a different font name and size accidentally, not to mention having a typo in from spelling something incorrectly.

You would also have to align the page numbers on the right side of the page. Stick with the Automatic table of contents and have the system generate it for you, error free.

Once you have chosen the style of TOC you like, your Table of Contents is automatically generated from the headings and styles you have used.

See how great this looks?

Table of Contents

What are the requirements for this course? ***1***

What am I going to get from this course? ***1***

Who is the target audience? ***1***

Correcting TOC Errors

Sometimes we get a little ahead of ourselves in our quest to get everything in our document put together. While we are writing away, sometimes we don't realize we clicked on the wrong style until a surprise shows up.

If you generate a table of contents and you discover graphics or other strange things where they don't belong, do not panic! These are very simple fixes.

For these examples, I will use a Table of Contents from one of my novels. My logo and my scene break icon do not belong in the table of contents, so let me show you how easy it is to fix this problem.

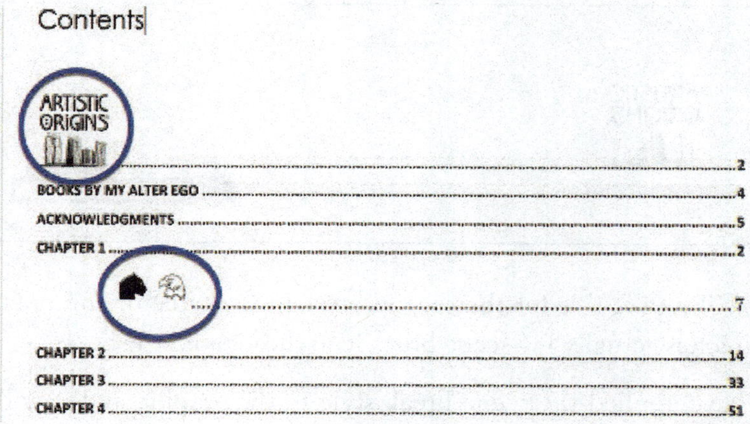

In the Table of Contents, click where the first surprise, my logo, showed up. In this example, I will click on the logo. That brings me to the page where it resides in the novel.

Now I will open the **Styles Pane** to see the styles in my book. When I click on the logo, I see that I accidentally chose **Book Title** instead of Logo.

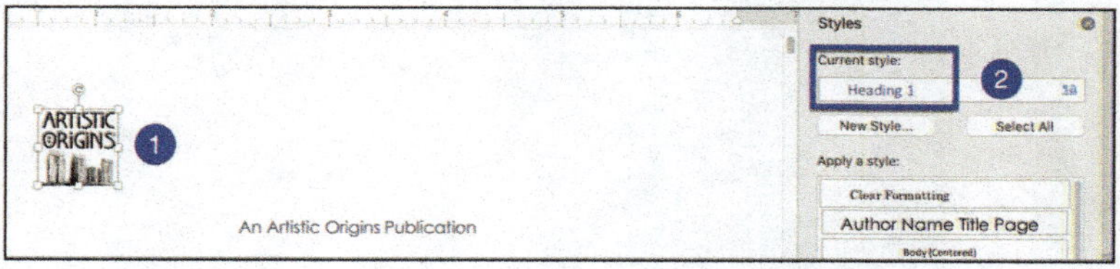

When I click on **Logo** in the Styles panel, the logo graphic will not show up in my table of contents when I regenerate it.

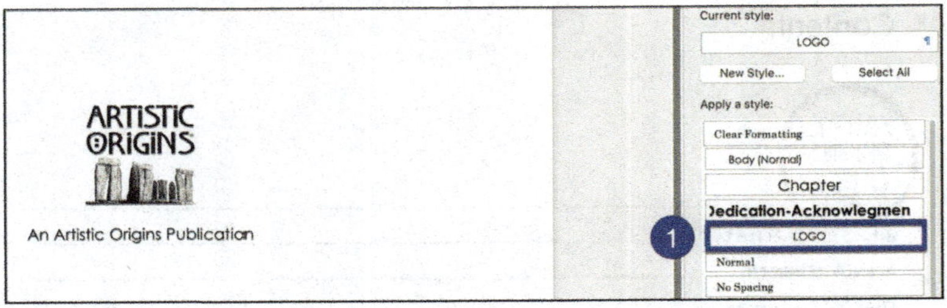

I will repeat this for the second error in the table of contents, which is actually my scene break icon throughout the book.

I have applied the scene break style to the graphic and it will not show up in the table of contents.

How to Regenerate the TOC

Just because I applied the new styles to the graphics that were in my TOC, they don't go away until I **re-generate** a whole new table of contents.

Highlight the entire table of contents.

Contents

While the TOC is highlighted, RIGHT-click using your mouse or track pad. The Update Field box will appear.

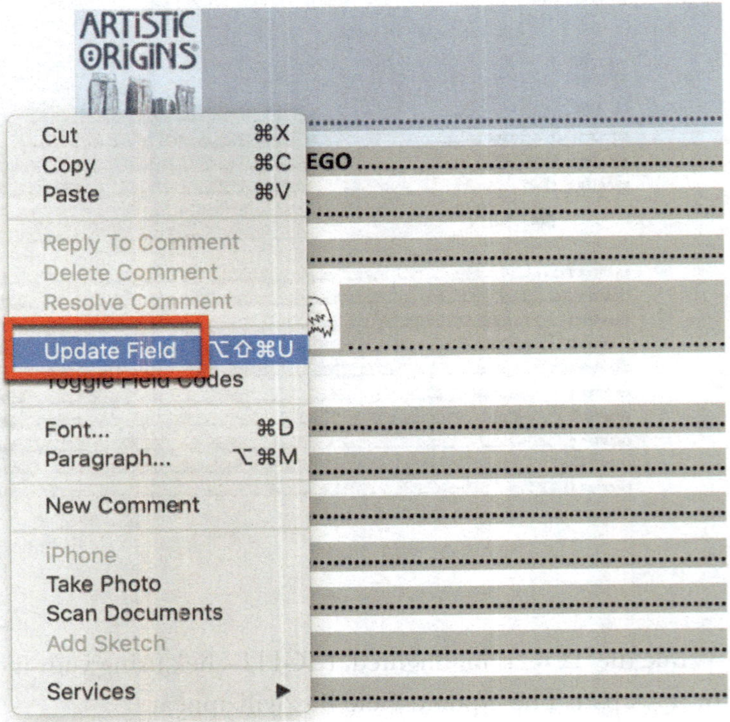

Click on Update Field.

You have two choices: **Update page numbers only**, and **Update entire table.**

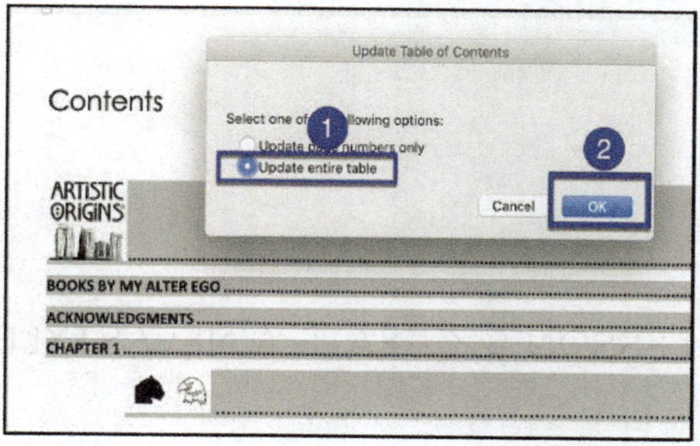

Click on **#1**, **Update entire table**.

Click **OK, #2**.

Everything is back to the way it should be, with no graphics or any other offending mistakes in the table of contents.

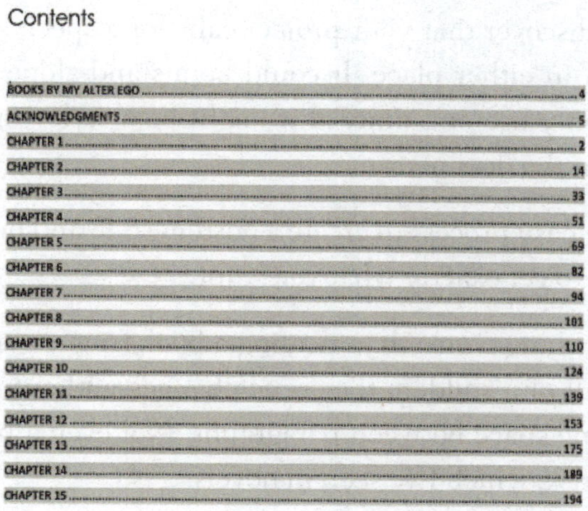
Contents

LESSON 5: CREATE A NEW STYLE

The Styles Pane and the panel that opens up below it, contains more styles than those listed in the Style Toolbar.

You may discover that your project calls for a special style that isn't listed in either place. It could be a stand-alone style that you will only use one time, or it might be a style you will use throughout the document.

It is a very easy process to create a custom style and only takes a few clicks to get exactly what you want.

There's nothing worse than reading a book from a giant glob of text and all of a sudden, the scene changes without any warning. No line space between paragraphs. Not even a pound sign or an asterisk, which I've seen in novels.

In my novels, I use a scene break to break up these changes.

How I Create My Scene Break Style

It is very, very easy to create a brand new Style. Let me show you how I do this.

Go to the Styles Pane.

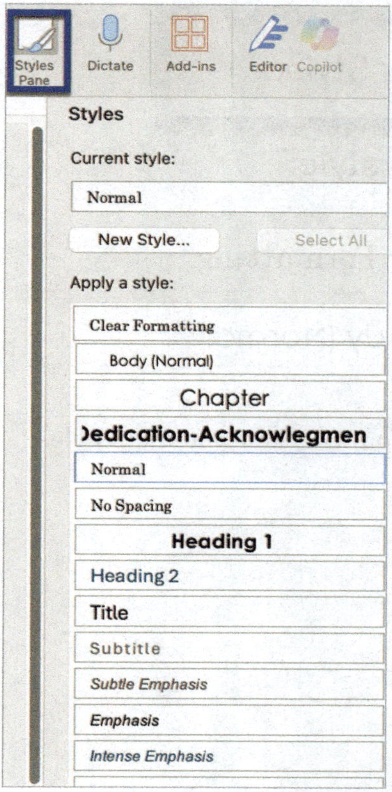

In the styles pane, click New Style.

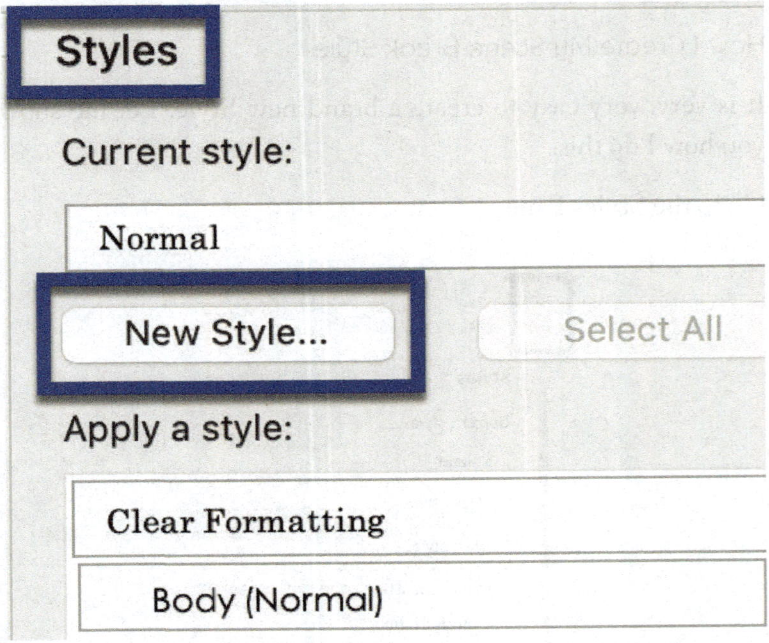

This is where you will name your new style.

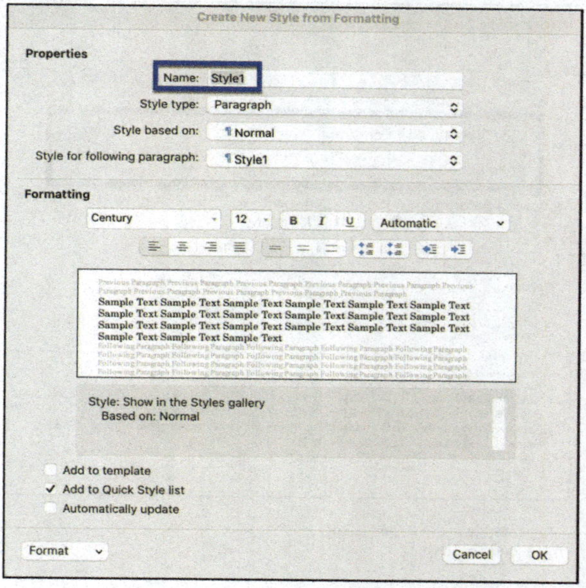

You can't name it something that has already been programmed as one of the AUTOMATIC STYLES, so come up with your own name.

For my purpose, I'm calling this Scene Break. I will type that in the Name field.

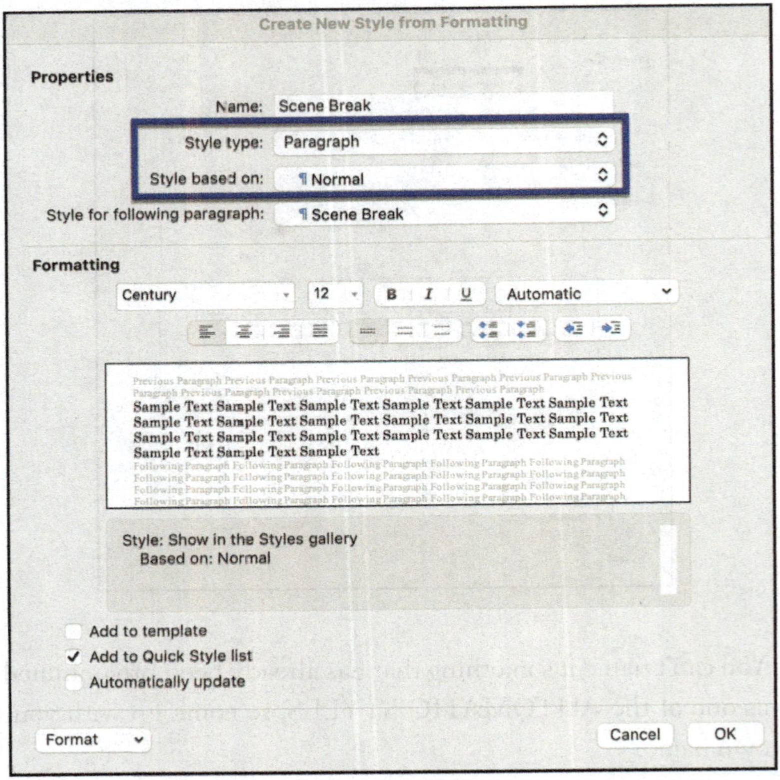

Beneath the Name field is the Style Type field, which shows Paragraph. That's what I want the paragraph following the scene break to be, so we will leave that alone.

The next field is Style Based On. The default is Normal.

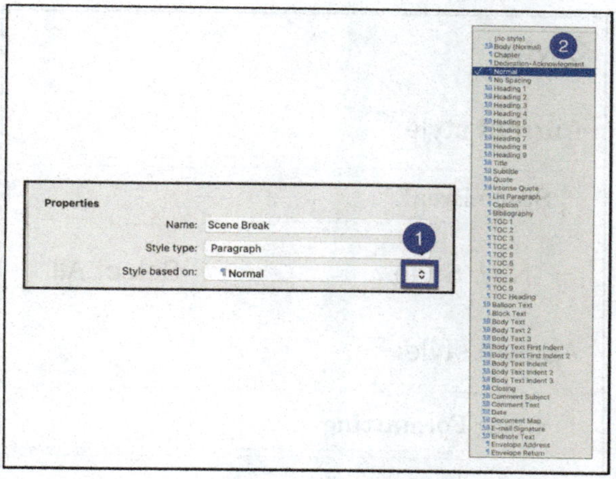

When you click on the Style Based On down arrow, #1 in this graphic, you will see all the choices to choose from in #2.

Unless you have a specific need, keep the default as Normal.

The Style for the following paragraph automatically populates with the Name you typed into the Name field.

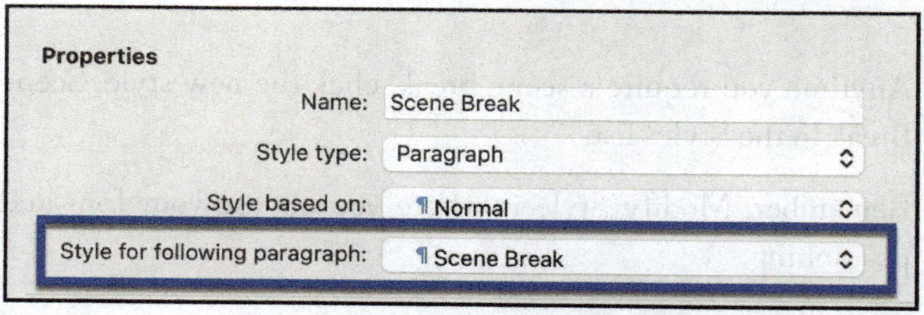

Use the down arrow to change the Style to Normal.

When you look at the Styles Pane, you will see your new style. In this example, you see Scene Break, what we created.

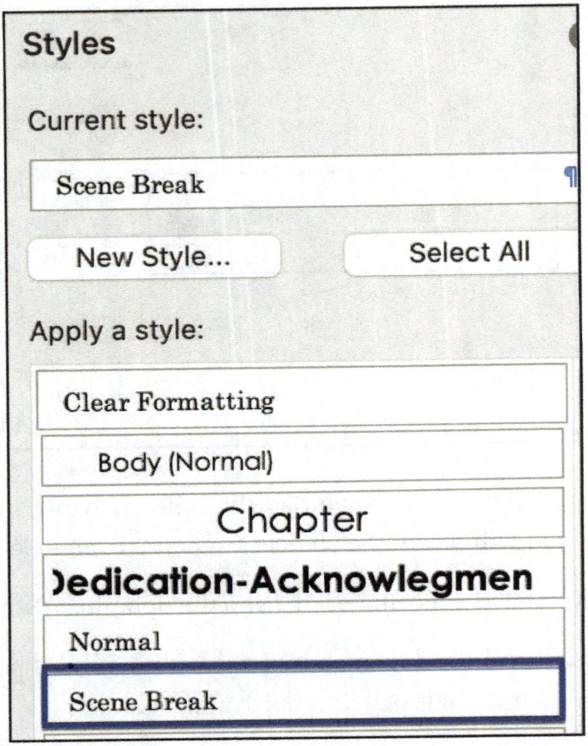

Anytime you require a scene break, click the new style, Scene Break in the Styles list.

Remember, Modify Style is where you choose your font and positioning.

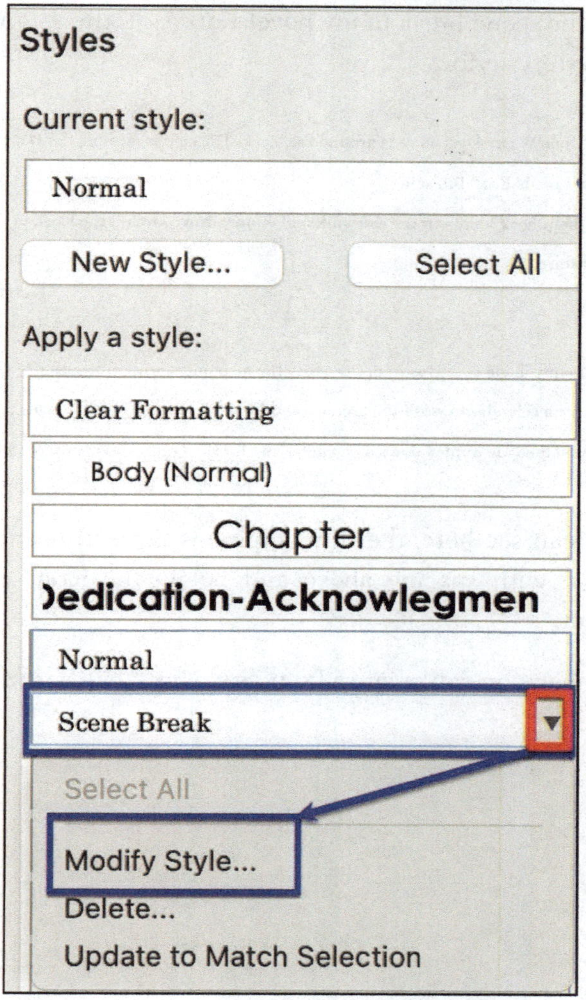

Since the icon for my scene break will be a tiny graphic, I have chosen Century size 10 for the font. I may have to adjust the size when I see it on the page of the book.

My scene breaks are always centered on the page, so I will set that up in Modify Style.

This is the scene break in my novel Katz' Cat, the Twinkle, TX cozy mystery series.

"Dime Water Food store is around the block. The sign is missing the D on Food so it reads Foo," Bill said.

They shook hands on the sidewalk and Jimmy drove around the block to the grocery store.

Jimmy made two trips from the car to the apartment with groceries. He hunted for a colander to wash the produce and finally found one stuck in a big pot in a lower cabinet. He hunted down a chopping mat for the veggies and fruit. He found

As you can see here, the tiny graphic is perfectly centered on the page with spacing above and below the icon so it will stand out.

Remember, you can create a New Style for whatever you need.

LESSON 6: CREATE A DOCUMENT TEMPLATE

In the corporate world, where I was a technical writer/editor for 34-years, organizations used templates to create all of their documents so they were uniform in style and they could be recognized at a glance.

A document template is very detailed. I will use examples from a template I created for a Fortune 500 company. Every single item that makes up a document will be set with a specific style.

Many times, templates get corrupted from being copied repeatedly, so a new one has to be created.

Check the Organization's Guidelines

Before you start on this project for your organization, check with your supervisor, HR, the marketing department, or the legal department to be sure that what you create is within the company's guidelines and policies for documentation.

Organizations typically have chosen specific fonts, sizes and colors for their documentation. And depending on what type of documentation you are creating, they may have different templates for each type. So, be sure to check before you plunge in and waste time.

Several departments work in conjunction with a graphic artist to develop the cover of a document. A graphic artist will create the image with guidance from others. You will instruct the artist so he knows what font name, size and color to use on the cover.

At first glance, the draft cover seems to look great.

When you dig into the company specifics, you realize the font should be Century Schoolbook 48, not Century Gothic 48. Also, the screenshot should be 3-1/2-inch square.

Here is a comparison of the cover images.

The correct cover with the organization's specific fonts, with the size and placement of the graphic, is on the left. You can see how easy it would be for someone to overlook the slight differences.

Always hover your cursor over things to see what the name and size of the font is to make sure it matches the specs of the template.

Creating Template Styles

Depending on the type of document you are creating this template for, the following styles may be used:

- Title
- Headings 1-3 or 4
- Normal
- Caption or figure caption
- Table title

There are dozens of styles already on hand in the Styles Panel. You may find just what you are looking for, or you may decide to modify one to your specific documentation needs.

You can control what styles you see in your document.

At the very bottom of the Styles Pane you will notice **List,** #1, with a drop-down menu.

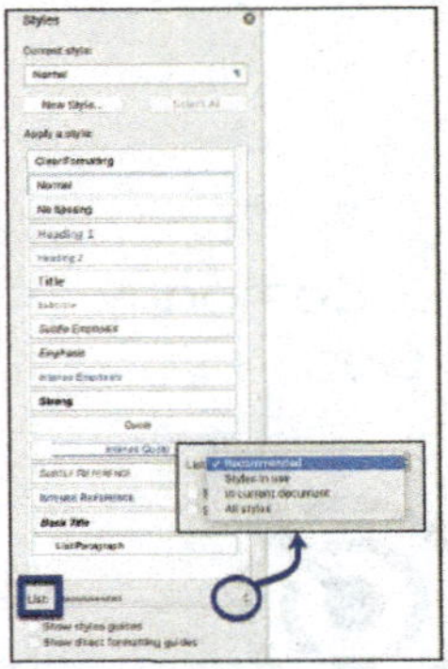

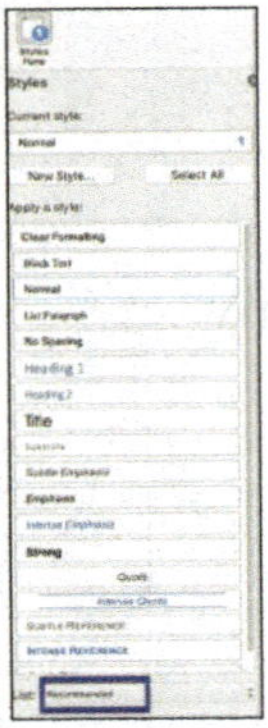

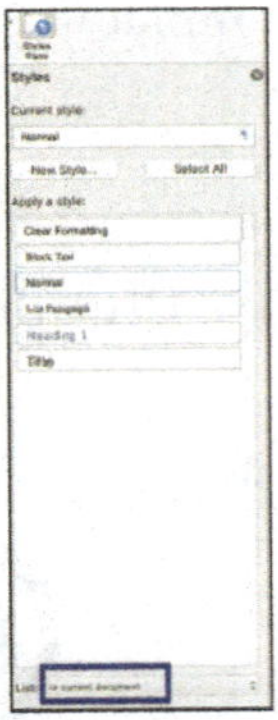

Click the arrow to see the following options:

- Recommended
- Styles in use
- In Current document
- All styles.

#2 shows the Styles in Use in the document. #3 shows the Styles in the current document.

As you begin your template with an open, blank Word document, click List at the bottom of the styles pane which is #1 in the screenshot, and choose **Styles in use**.

The current style is Normal, #2.

Clear Formatting is listed in the pane #3.

Clear Formatting is a **function**, not a style. This is useful for clearing out the formatting when you applied the wrong style.

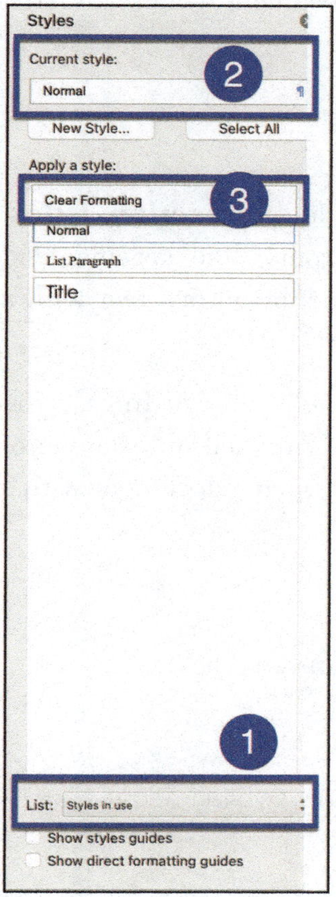

To clear the formatting you recently applied, highlight the text and click clear formatting. It will return to the default.

Be aware that if you selected your entire document contents with Select All, then choose clear formatting, every style you have applied will be wiped out, back to the original defaults.

However, if you want to clear formatting you applied to a particular section of your document, highlight only that text and click clear formatting and it will return to the default.

Title Setup

As you can see in this example, this client chose HelveticaNeue Condensed as their corporate font.

Titles are set using that font in an18 point size. The Table of Contents is built with Titles, and may include Chapter titles, Section titles or both.

The frontmatter pages, which make up the copyright ownership, legal statements and other information, will be numbered using Roman numerals, such as i, ii, etc.

All document page numbers will be in the standard Arabic format of 1, 2, 3.

The paragraph, or body text in this document will use an Arial 12 font.

Headings

Headings are applied to **chapter** and/or **section titles**. Each level is built using specific fonts, line spacing, and whether the section title is bold, italic, or normal text with a specific size and font name.

Most documents use two or three heading styles. In case you have to use a fourth heading, I have supplied an example of available headings. Rarely have I ever seen a document with a fifth level heading.

1 First Level Heads – Heading 1

First level headings start on a new page using Heading 1 which will use HelveticaNeue 18, with 12 points after the heading and before body/paragraph text begins.

1.1 Second Level Heading

Second heading will use HelveticaNeue 16 bold and italic with 12 points before and after the heading so as not to crowd paragraph/body text.

1.1.1 Third Level Heading

Third level heading is HelveticaNeue 14 with 12 points before and after the heading.

1.1.1.1 Fourth Level Heading

Fourth level heading is HelveticaNeue 14 bold italic with 12 points before and after text.

First Level Heads – Heading 1

The client has specified that first level heads will begin on a new page using a left justified Heading 1.

The spacing will be set with 12 points after the heading and before the body or paragraph text begins.

Notice that Heading 1 in the screenshot appears to be centered When you click on Heading 1, select Modify to change all the specifics to what is required for your client document.

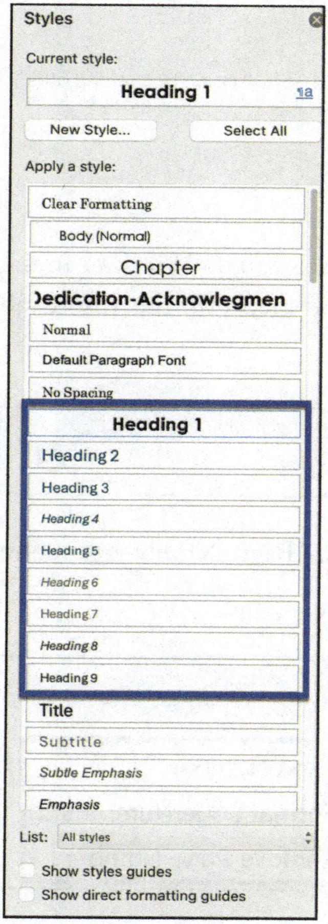

Each heading type will have to be modified with the correct specs from your client's template choices.

As you can see here, second, third and fourth headings use different size fonts and attributes. Some use bold and italic fonts, and specific spacing before and after the headings.

Choose Modify Style for all Headings

1.1 Second Level Headings

Second level heads use HelveticaNeue 16 bold and italic with 12 points before and after the heading so as not to crowd the body text.

1.1.1 Third Level Headings

Third level heads are HelveticaNeue 14 with 12 points before and after the heading.

1.1.1.1 Fourth Level Heading

Fourth level heads are HelveticaNeue 14 bold italic with 12 points before and after the heading.

Page Numbers

Page numbers are included on the Insert tab on Word, #1 in the screenshot. Slide your eyes across the menu on the Insert tab and you will find #2, Page Number.

When you click the down arrow on Page Number, a menu opens, #3 in the graphic.

For some reason, both Page Number and Format Page Number open the same box. Don't ask me why, I'm not the programmer. Either way, that box is where you choose the position and alignment for your page numbers.

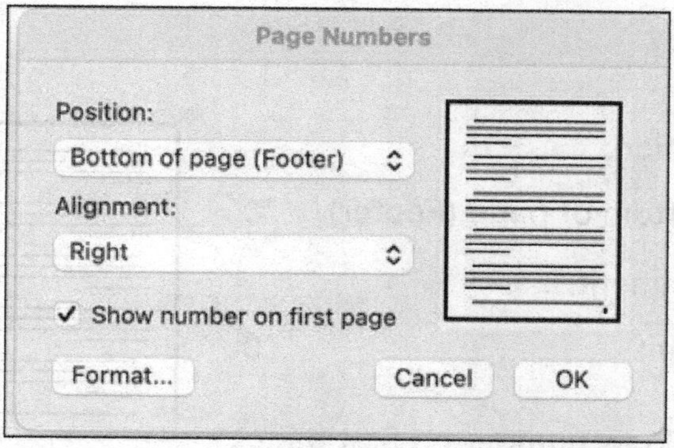

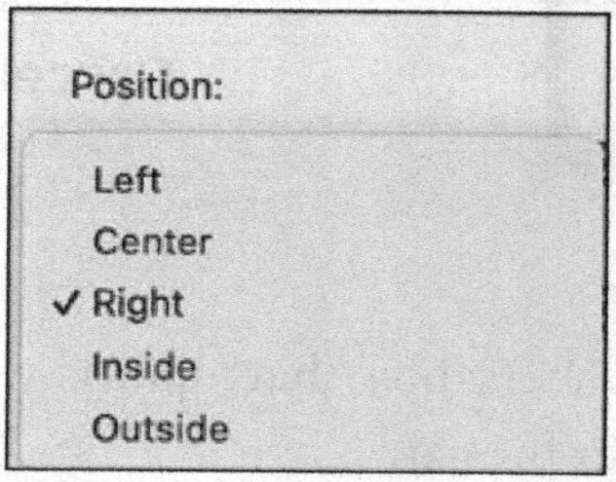

Position: Top of the page (Header), or Bottom of the page (Footer).

Alignment: Left, Center, Right, Inside, Outside.

At the bottom of the Page Numbers box, click on Format. This will take you to the screen where you will be able to choose your numbering style.

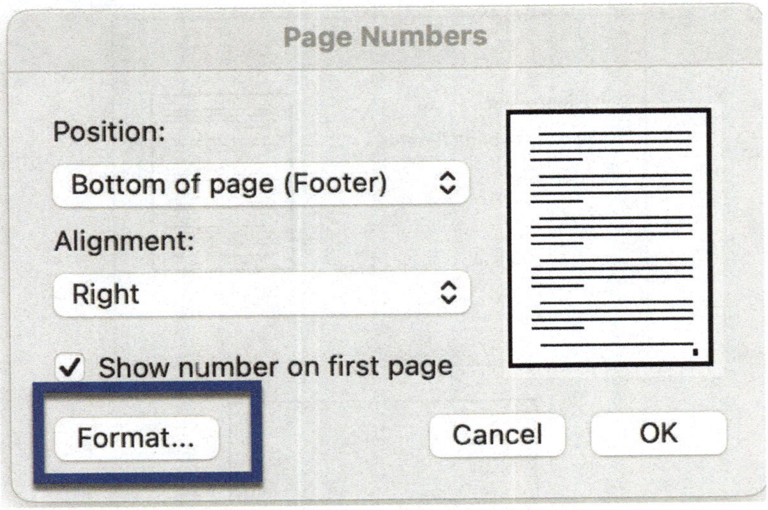

On the Page Numbers box that opens, you will be able to choose your number format.

Roman numbers are i, ii numbers. They are typically used for the frontmatter of books. You will also find that some books use them in a bibliography and reference sections in the back of the book.

Arabic numbers – those regular numbers, 1, 2, 3, are used for the body of the book.

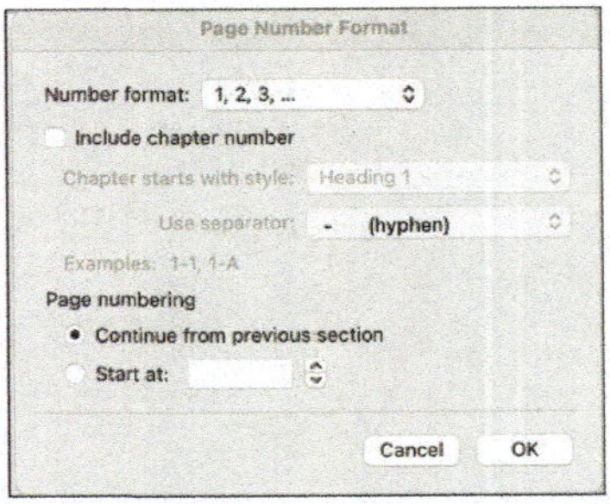

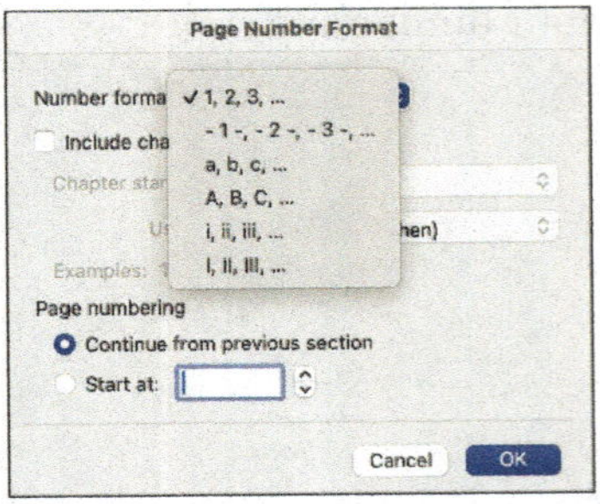

In the Page Numbers box you also have options to include your chapter numbers.

On the bottom of the Page Numbers box, you will be able to choose whether you want the page numbers to start at a specific number, other than page 1, or to continue from a previous section.

Lists, Bullets, and Tables

Numbered or bulleted lists are always set up so that the number is indented with aligned indented text that follows.

Sometimes lists are created in table format so they don't spill onto more pages. It looks a lot better when they can spill across a page in formatted splendor.

When you create a table that will include a bulleted or numbered list, decide whether the box will be visible or invisible. If the box is visible, you will want to check with corporate as to what the line color and width should be.

In this example, the lines are 25% gray. They show up, but not glaringly so if they had been black.

• Text	• Text
• Text	• Text
• Text	• Text

Figures, screenshots, drawings, photos—whatever you call the graphic, should ALWAYS have the caption UNDER the picture to include the figure number and title.

Always leave adequate space before and after a drawing so the text doesn't crowd the picture. For this client, I used the standard 3 blank lines before the drawing, and 3 blank lines after the caption under the picture.

Depending on the type of screenshot, there may or may not be a box around it.

Screenshots, figures and graphics will be centered on the page and will have a minimum of three blank lines before, and 3 blank lines after the screenshot and Figure title. Screenshots/graphics will be proportionate to their size and function.

There may or may not be a box around the figure.
1 blank line
2 blank line
3 blank line

Figure x.x: Figure title

1 blank line
2 blank line
3 blank line
Text resumes here.

When you are creating a regular table, after you determine the size of the table you require, you should also think about placement on the page.

Will the table be centered, or is it so large that it will span the width of the page?

Add at a minimum 2 blank lines before and after the table to give it distance from the previous or following text.

In this example, the outside border and the inside lines are 40% gray.

The table title always goes ABOVE the table and should be aligned to the edge of the table, not at the left paragraph.

When the table spills over onto another page, always include the table title, a comma, then the word Continued **in italic** and one size smaller than the title.

Table Title, ***Continued***

Bold Centered Text	**Bold Centered Text**
Left aligned text	**Left aligned text**

In the event you do not know how to italicize something, follow these easy directions.

- Highlight the word or content you want italicized
- Click on the *I* in the toolbar (see screenshot)
- Your word or content becomes italicized

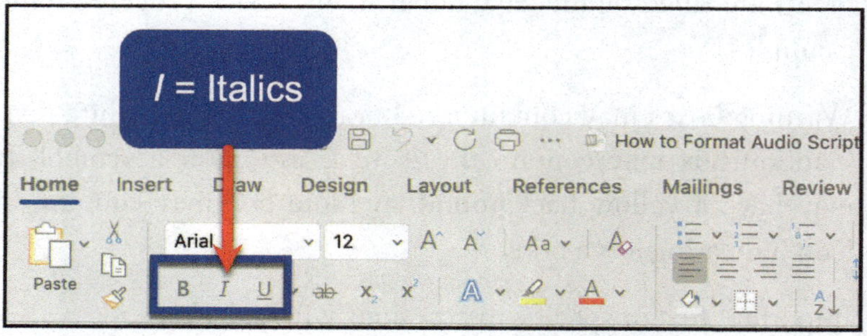

Warnings, Cautions, and Notes

Depending on your industry and the type of document you are creating the template for, you may have a need for warning, caution, or note boxes or statements.

It is extremely important that you check with your legal department for the wording that will create these boxes or statements.

There is a legal difference between the words **may, shall** and **will**. Find out which words you should use in each specific instance.

You will be able to find different symbols to show whether the box or statement contains a warning, caution or note. Some companies have their own symbols; others use OSHA-approved symbols that are widely recognized. Many companies use ANSI symbols now, especially if they work internationally. There are also ISO-approved screenshot symbols for most industries.

Check with your legal, or other department to determine what type of symbols your company requires.

Warning, Caution, and Note boxes should have two blank lines before the box begins and two blank lines after. These statements are ruled by the legal department. I have provided some examples.

Warning boxes may contain a red background with white text. Caution box may contain the word Caution, or a symbol. It may have a yellow background. A Note box may contain an icon indicating it is a note.

Important text or specific instructions will be **bold**.

WARNING	**Warning** indicates imminent danger of personnel injury or death if warning is not carefully observed or followed.
CAUTION	**Caution** indicates potential danger of personnel injury or death if caution is not carefully observed or followed.
	**Note** indicates additional information to correctly perform an action.

Some documents require a Glossary or an Acronym list. Place those in the back of the document in the appendix.

A glossary does not contain abbreviations or acronyms.

GLOSSARY

Term	Definition
Do-hickey	A thing-a-ma-jig.

ACRONYM LIST

Acronym	Definition
OSHA	Occupational Safety and Health Administration of the United States Department of labor, formed by the Occupational safety and Health Act of 1970.

Superscript and Subscript

Superscript is useful for building a bibliography of references, which also goes into the appendix at the back of the book.

When used in this form, the superscript would follow text with a superscript number[14] above the word.

When used as a reference indicator, the reference may sometimes be found at the bottom of the page; other times, you will find a bibliography of references in the back of the document.

Subscript is used for typing chemical compounds, such as N_2, the formula for nitrogen.

You can find these tools in the toolbar on the Home tab in Word.

Superscript is indicated with an X with the number 2 over it. Subscript is indicated with an X with the number 2 below it.

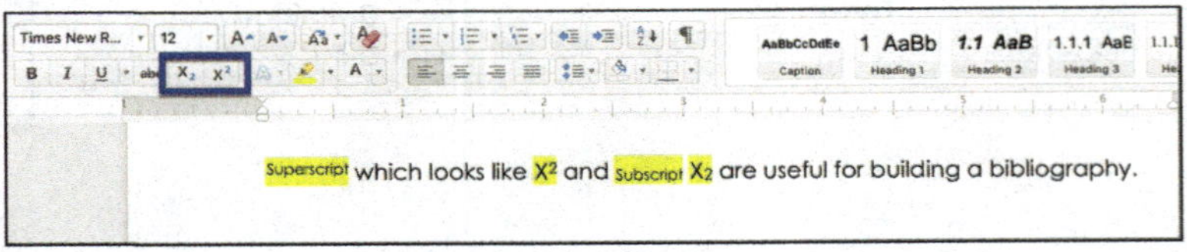

LESSON 7: YOUR FRIEND THE PILCROW MARK

Everyone needs a best friend. In Microsoft Word, the Pilcrow mark, also called a backwards letter P, or a paragraph mark, will fill that spot, many times over.

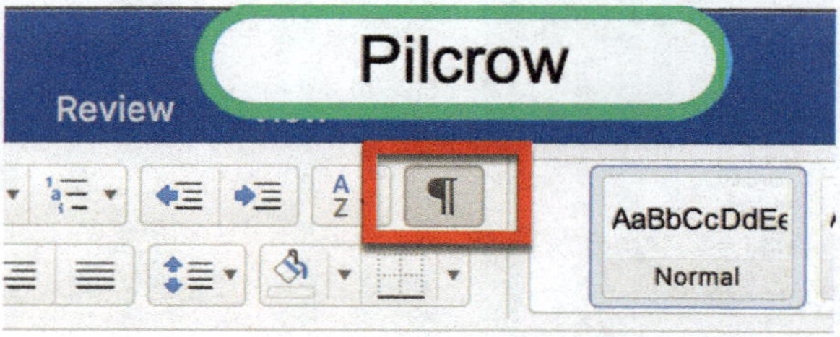

According to Keith Houston of ShadyCharacters.co.UK, the pilcrow was given life by Aristophanes of Byzantium, librarian of the great institution at Alexandria in the 3rd century BC. If you are a history buff, check out his website.

Finding Problems in Your Documents

The following document looks like one big mess. If you blindly click around to fix things, you end up with a bigger mess.

You want to write a book, but you don't know the first thing about getting started. Will it cost you money to create a book? How should you begin? Maybe you're not that computer
savvy. This course helps you get everything organized so when you sit down in front of that computer you will not be intimidated by the setup and mechanics of getting started. You will be able to dive into writing your book content and, you will make great progress as you challenge yourself to write more and more each time you sit down at your computer. The great thing is, you will learn some neat tips and tricks along the way to make your book dream come true.

Some of the things you will learn are:

- Why you should test the waters with an eBook
- How to organize your new writing business
- How to make project folders and subfolders
- How to protect your work and your computer equipment
- Why you should research characters' professions
- How to know your locations if you live somewhere else
- How to set up your working file
- What are Styles?
- Don't do that manually!
- Where is that thing?
- Why join a Critique Group

What are the requirements for this course?

First and foremost, you should have the desire to write a book. While you can use a pen and paper, it is highly advisable to use a computer with a word processing program because writing the book is only the first part of your journey.

What am I going to get from this course?

This
course
will
prepare
you so
you can
sit down
and
begin
the
organiz
ation of
your
book
and
start
writing.
Who is
the
target
audienc
e?
This course is for anyone who has an idea for a book, or someone who has already written a book but it has been sitting in a drawer on hold because they didn't know what they were doing. And anyone who needs a refresher course.

When you click the pilcrow mark, #1, the paragraph symbols show up in the document, along with tiny dots that are spacers between words.

For this example, if you notice the pilcrow mark at the end of the word computer, #2, you see that an accidental Return broke up the paragraph. This little typo caused one of the problems.

The next problem, #3, shows the tabs moved from the flush left position just a smidgen which caused the lines of text under the word computer to be indented, #4.

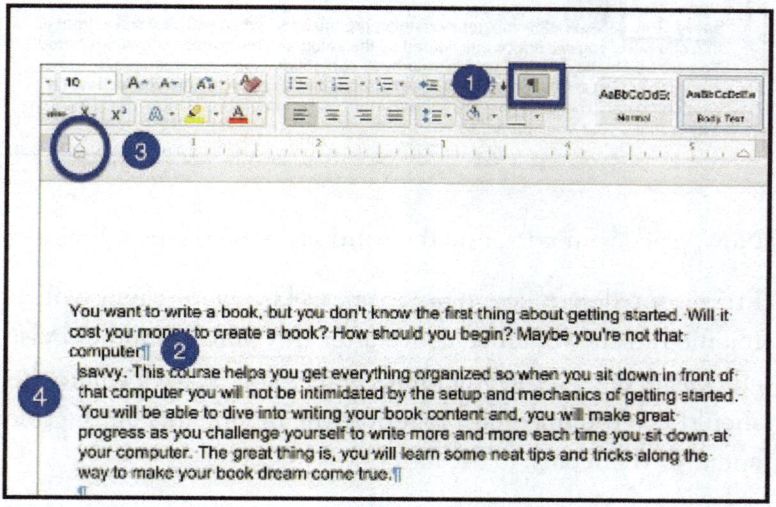

Instead of freaking out about a mess in your document, if you slow down and study the problem in your document, the solution may be staring back at you.

In this case, this will be a very easy fix that only takes a few clicks to sort out.

First, place your cursor after the word computer, before the pilcrow mark #1. Add 1 blank space.

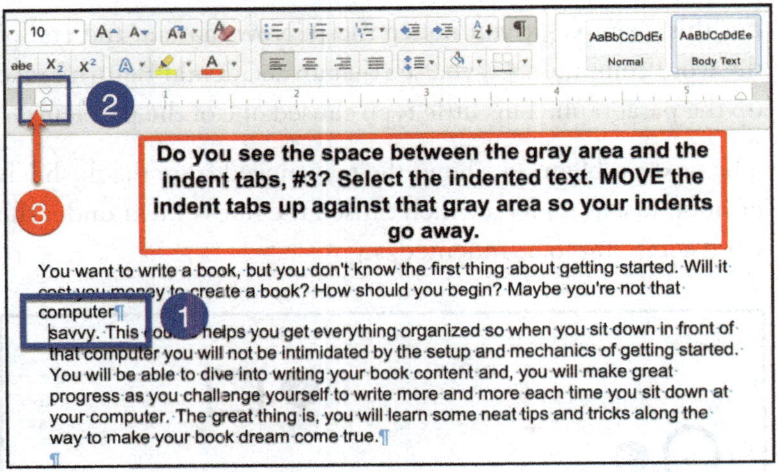

Now, place your cursor on the word savvy on the next line.

Press your delete key 1 or 2 times. The word savvy will be rejoined in the sentence above after the word computer. Visually check that all the other lines of text will be back where they should be. You may have to adjust the tab indents on the ruler and drag them back to the left.

The only things you should see on the screen are the paragraph marks and spacers between words—**one dot only between words**.

In this example, delete the extra dots so your spacing doesn't show gaps between words.

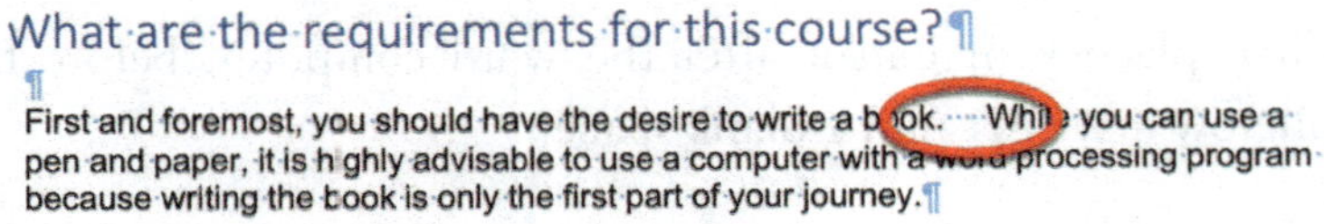

Always edit documents with the pilcrow mark highlighted (on) to catch errors.

This next example is from my novel Hot Chocolate. I wanted you to see how the scene break icon, which is a rolling pin, is perfectly centered on the page with the appropriate line spacing above and below it.

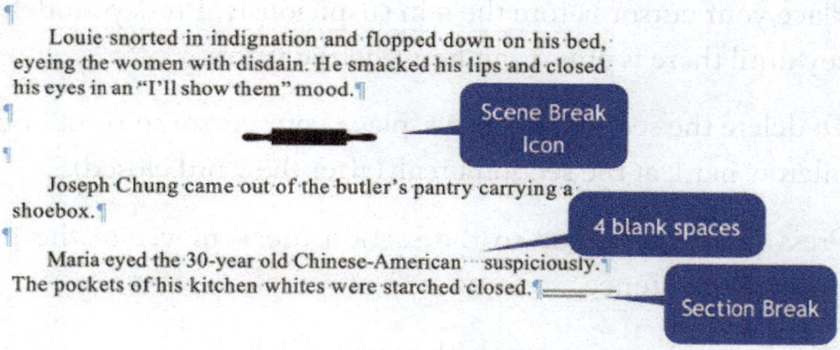

Did you notice there seems to be a big gap between words a couple of sentences under the scene break? There are four blank spaces. Three of them have to be deleted.

The next problem is a section break. I don't know why it is there, but that's getting deleted so the words flow from page to page. There wasn't any reason for the section break

If you are writing a book, you or your editor should always check your document with the pilcrow mark highlighted to catch errors prior to printing or uploading your book.

When writing corporate documents, you should make sure your documents are free from mistakes, many of which are hidden unless you highlight your pilcrow mark.

Here's another example of things you normally would not catch without the Pilcrow mark.

There are 3 or 4 extra spaces (tiny dots) #1 here between these two words where there should only be 1 tiny dot.

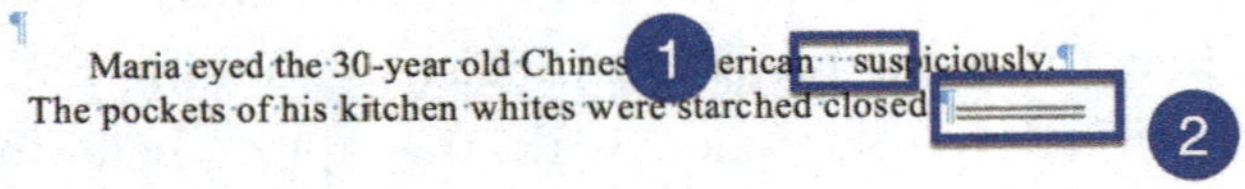

Place your cursor before the **s** in suspiciously. Press your delete key until there is only 1 dot between the words.

To delete the section break, #2, place your cursor in front of the pilcrow mark at the section break (after the word closed).

Press your return key so the section break moves to the line below the sentence.

Highlight the section break, then press Delete.

That's it, folks

You've come to the end of my How to Format Word Docs Like a Pro.

Thanks for joining me to learn about these little mysteries. If this book has helped you in your day-to-day life, please send me a message and let me know.

I hope you join me again when I have other tidbits of information you can use to make your working life easier.

Please leave a review. I want to hear from you about your experiences with this book. I appreciate your comments. If you have complaints, I want to hear about them so I can make improvements to this content.

Everything you've ever wanted to know about me is on my website: degreenfield.com

Sign up for my free newsletter. You'll be able to find out when I have a new class.

I'm gifting you a bonus of my How to use Track Changes guide that I created for my clients.

Most people who use Microsoft Word have never heard of Track Changes. It is a very handy tool when you send a document out for review to get comments back. People will be able to read your document and make comments, delete and add text or graphics.

This guide will instruct you on how to use Track Changes.

LESSON 8: GUIDE TO TRACK CHANGES

Track Changes is a handy tool when you need comments on a document from a team of people, or just a pal. Each person can add their comments and you will see their name on the right side of the page with their comments or edits.

Depending on your version of MS Word, the toolbar you see in these screenshots may not be in the same place in your version of the program.

Track Changes is typically under the **Review** tab when you open a Word doc.

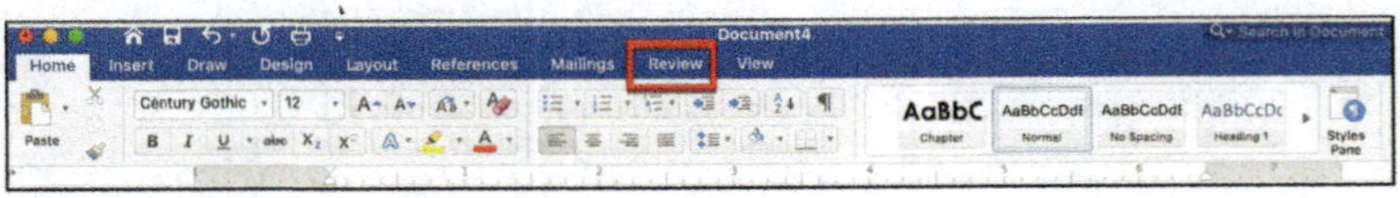

Click on the Review tab in the toolbar. It will open to this screen where you will see **Tracking**.

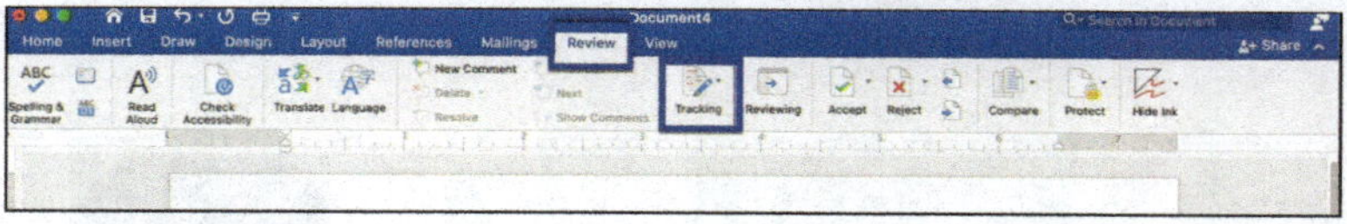

Click on the down arrow beside **Tracking**. The following menu opens.

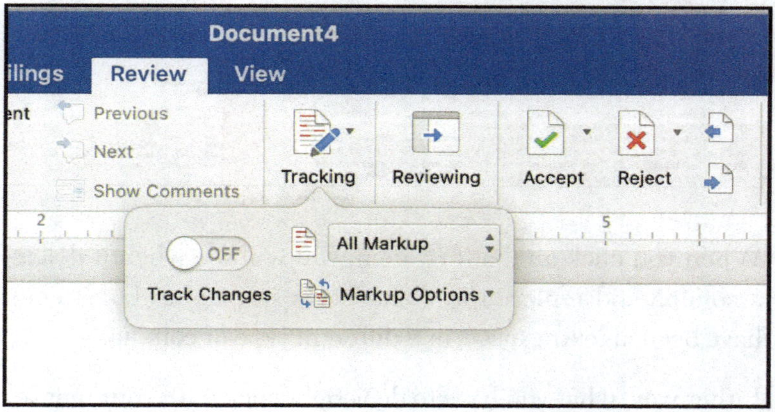

Click the button OFF so it turns to **ON**. It will turn green.

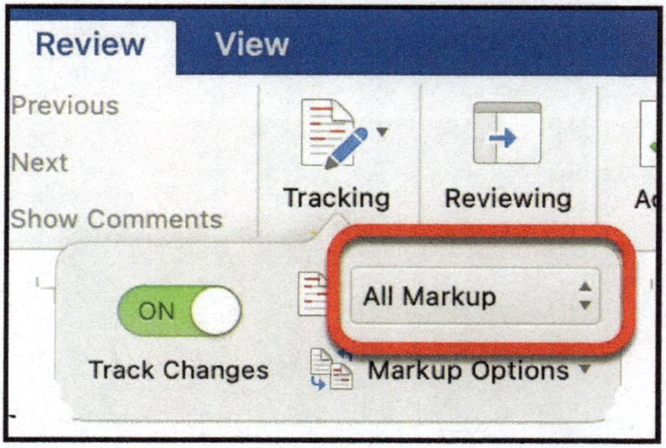

Now you are ready to look at all the changes and how to process them.

Work in the column on the right.

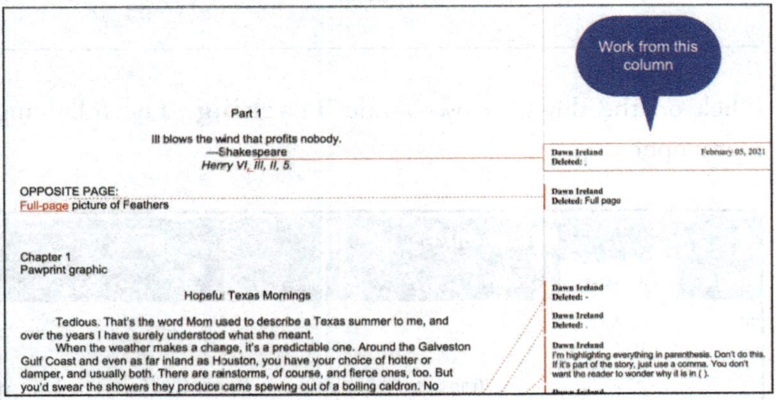

When you click on that first item, you will see where I deleted a comma and replaced it. That seems suspicious, but it could have been an extra space, or a different type of comma.

Either way, what you have to do is right click with your mouse.

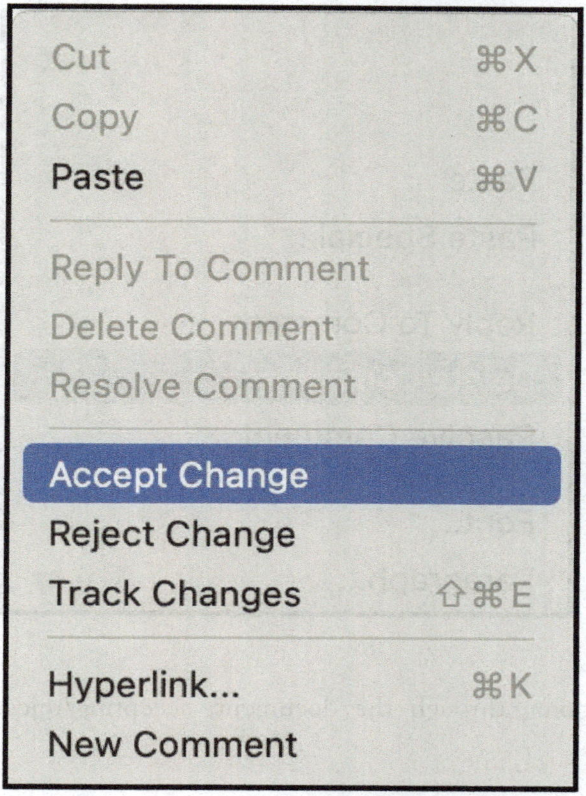

If you do not agree with something, click **Reject** instead of **Accept**.

When you come across a comment in the right column, you can **Reply to Comment**, **Delete Comment**, or **Resolve Comment**.

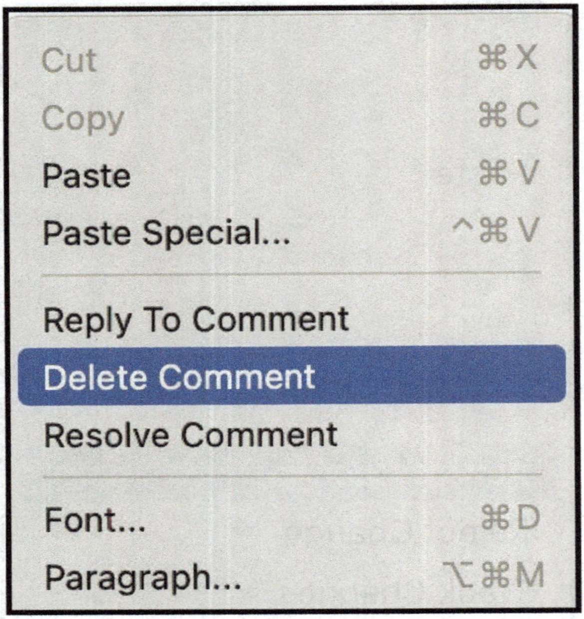

Keep going through the document, accepting/rejecting the redlines.

If you come across something that you can't seem to make go away, turn on the Pilcrow mark to identify the problem. If you can't find the problem, send me an email and I'll try to help.

LESSON 9: SIMPLE IMAGE RESIZER INSTRUCTIONS

Here's a little extra bonus. Many people want to use images and don't know how to work with them. This is an easy program that lets you resize images so they work better in your document, on your website, or anywhere you need a specific size of an image.

Simple Image Resizer is a free program you can access here:

http://www.simpleimageresizer.com/upload#.YcZQHy-B3z8

The instructions are easy to follow, and I have X'd through junk that you **should not click**.

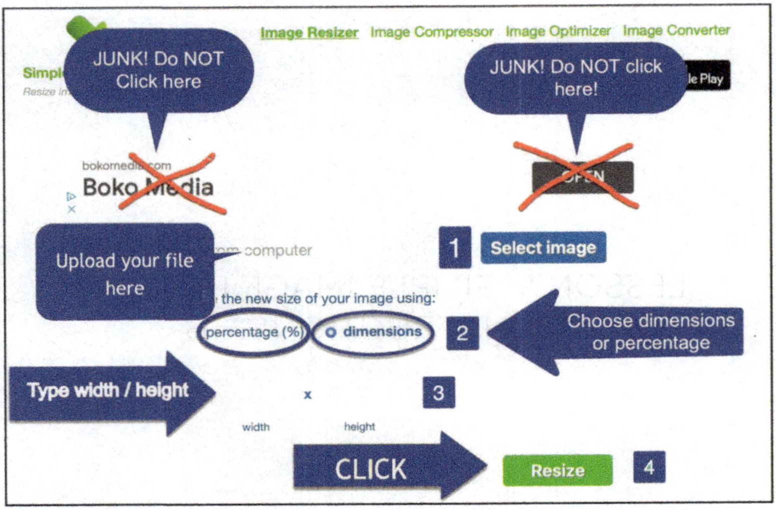

#1 – Select your image from your computer.

#2 – Choose **dimensions** unless you know the exact percentage.

#3 – Type the **width** and the **height**.

#4 – Click **Resize**.

When you upload your JPEG, do not be alarmed when you see **C:\fakepath**the name of your file JPEG, as shown in the next image.

It only takes seconds for the conversion.

Then **click Download**.

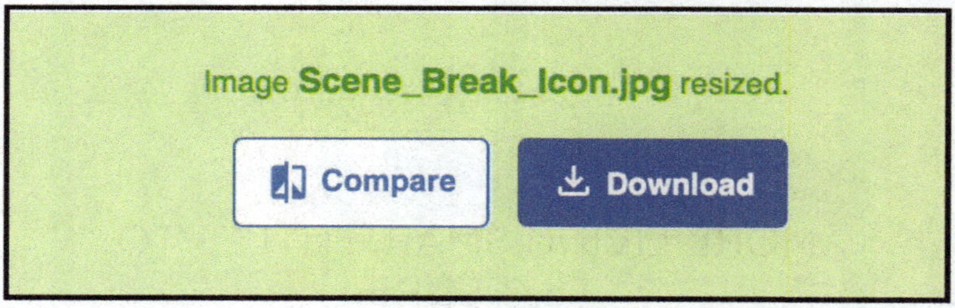

Be sure to pay attention to **where** you have downloaded the image (file name and folder).

That's all there is to it. Now you have a free source to resize your images for each application.

MORE LIVING SMART TITLES TO EXPLORE

Get smarter, learn easier. You might want to check out more of my Living Smart books. The whole point is to make your life easier.

Writers Preparation Handbook

You want to write a book, but you don't know the first thing about getting started. Will it cost you money to create a book? How should you begin? Maybe you're not that computer savvy.

This book helps you get everything organized so when you sit down in front of that computer you will not be intimidated by the setup and mechanics of getting started.

You will be able to dive into writing your book content and, you will make great progress as you challenge yourself to write more and more each time you sit down at your computer.

The great thing is, you will learn some neat tips and tricks along the way to make your book dream come true.

Some of the things you will learn are:

- Why you should test the waters with an eBook
- Organize your new writing business
- Make project folders and subfolders
- Protect your work and your computer equipment
- Research characters' professions
- Know your locations
- Setting up your working file
- Learn and use Styles
- Don't do that manually!
- Where is that thing?
- Critique Groups

What are the requirements?

First and foremost, you should have the desire to write a book. While you can use a pen and paper, it is highly advisable to use a computer with a word processing program because writing the book is only the first part of your journey.

Check out the online course which is identical to this book.

https://www.dawngreenfieldireland.com/online-courses

Mastering Your Money 2022 Edition

Mastering Your Money 2022 Edition by award-wining author Dawn Greenfield Ireland will take the mystery out of why transactions bounce.

The original MYM was created in 2007, and won the New England Book Festival competition in its category in 2008.

This book is perfect for people starting out on their own, high school and college students, anyone recovering from a divorce or tragic ending of a relationship where they are thrust into the role of responsibility for their household.

You will learn:

- How to create a budget
- National Averages of expenses to see where you fit in
- How to fill out a blank check
- How to read a bank statement
- How to avoid double payments, forgetting to make a payment
- What happens to late payments
- Why checks bounce (you contribute to this)
- What happens when checks bounce
- Banking Statistics & Facts
- How to make your checkbook your financial guru
- Understand how to maintain your checkbook so you can safely use online banking without disasters
- And a whole lot more

Multiple licenses and discounts are available for corporate, educational, or training purposes. Your logo can go on the cover.

What's Breaking Your Budget?

When you're drowning in debt and can't see how you can turn things around, it's time to examine what's really going on in your life. Not all budgets are equal. Many only hit the top common living expenses.

What's Breaking Your Budget dives deep into your habits. Things you may not want to admit to that are breaking you down and making a mess of your life. This book will thoroughly help you explore all outgoing cash in all forms, many of which you don't even consider as an expense until the money's gone.

You will learn how to create a true budget from the work you be guided through in the book. Once you complete the process, you will be able to breathe easier and begin to eliminate your debt once and for all.

Nonfiction	
The Puppy Baby Book	Mastering Your Money (2022)
Puppy Adoption and Beyond	Writers Preparation Handbook
Mastering Your Money (2008)	What's Breaking Your Budget
Online Classes	
Writers Preparation Handbook	How to Format Word Docs Like A Pro
Cozy Mysteries	**Sci-Fi-Fantasy**
The Alcott Family Adventures	**The Thol Series**
Hot Chocolate	Prophecy of Thol
Bitter Chocolate	Gifts From Thol
Spicy Chocolate	Love of Thol
Nutty Chocolate	King of Thol
Katz' Cat Series	Earth Calling Thol
Katz' Cat	**Sci-Fi Romance Adventure**
Bill Hill's Pills	Forced Dreams
The Detectives	**Dystopian**
The Pact	The Last Dog
	Texmexzona
Books by my Alter Ego ~ DG Ireland	
Bonded Shapeshifter Billionaire Series	
Bonded	
Tothars	
Tilted	
Unforeseen	
Connected	
Need A Notebook?	
See my 54 themed notebooks on my website www.degreenfield.com/notebooks	
Screenplays formatted as books	
Plan B (Dark Comedy)	Where's Ralphie? (Family Comedy)
The God Child (Action Adventure)	Standing Dead (Drama/Tragedy)
The Far Corner (Sci-Fi/Psychological/Creatures)	
Screenplays as TV Episodes	
Hot Chocolate ~ Episode 1	Prophecy of Thol ~ Episode 1
Bonded ~ Episode 1	
See my screenplays and awards on my website: degreenfield.com Filmfreeway, ISA Network	

ABOUT THE AUTHOR

Thanks for joining me to learn about these little mysteries. If this book has helped you in your day-to-day life, please send me a message and let me know.

I hope you join me again when I have other tidbits of information you can use to make your working life easier.

Visit my website when you have a chance. Sign up for my free newsletter. You'll be able to find out when I have a new class.

https://degreenfield.com

Dawn Greenfield Ireland writes full time. She lives among dreams and fantasies with two cats and moving boxes. Her head is filled with stories. She doesn't suffer from writer's block.

If you buy her books and products, she'll love you forever.

How about leaving a review on your favorite retailer? Reviews help authors so much.

facebook.com/dawn.ireland.18
x.com/dawnireland
instagram.com/dawngreenfieldIreland
goodreads.com/dawnireland
linkedin.com/dawnireland
tiktok.com/@writerg4l

Made in the USA
Monee, IL
03 November 2026

67379457R00056